PROBLEM POOCH BOOK 2: STRESSED TO SERENE

CAROL CLARK

PROBLEM POOCH TO PERFECT PET
Book 2
STRESSED TO SERENE

Find out how to help your fearful, stressed or naughty dog; why they develop
various fears, the common stresses dogs suffer, why some dogs are so noisy - and
what to do to help them

Carol Clark
The Doggy Doctor

To my brother, Peter. I miss you.

Also to Vicky and the Moxie crew for the support and encouragement and to all the owners who allow me to help them and their dogs

Your stories give me the ideas for my books. Thank you.

TESTIMONIALS

Another good one from Carol! I thoroughly enjoyed reading this book. It provides the perfect mixture of education and entertainment. The intro to the individual behaviours that are being discussed is provided by a true case summary and yes, I did recognise a few of the issues other dog owners are having in our own dog. This made me instantly feel better and I was eager to read on what could be done about it.

Included with the vast amount of training tips, management options and scientific information, the reader gets many "laugh out loud moments" to avoid being sucked into a problem bubble. I certainly had a few sideways looks from my husband, questioning: "I thought you are reading a book about behaviour problems in dogs, what is there to laugh about?!"

The writing style is so down to earth, easy to read, the book is jam packed with information and I cannot wait for the next one!

Sandra D, dog owner

Very readable style. I liked the chatty and anecdotal quality. Your writing has a warm and approachable style which made me want to read on. I quite enjoyed the scientific detail behind human and canine behaviour and the link between the two species but have to confess, not having a scientific background, I skipped bits. I liked the real-life examples of behavioural problems and the context. I loved the little line drawings.

The summary at the end of each section was very useful. It was good to read what I was supposed to have taken out of the chapter, go back and re-read.

Wendy H, author (aka Georgia Hill)

Generally an excellent book, well written, funny in parts but very apt examples and relevant information. It was interesting from start to finish and we could so identify with it in many places. We really enjoyed reading it and couldn't wait to get to the section on barking which was very helpful. We could almost hear your voice in the book. Loved your honesty about Gus and the mistakes you made. We wish we had read it when Sam was a puppy.

Gary & Beverley N, dog owners

I love Carol's writing. The humour makes it a pleasure to read even where there are emotionally quite difficult subjects being discussed. The case studies show the problems in real life, as it were, and the tips for how these dogs can be helped will prove invaluable if you've got a dog with the problem.

Anne P, dog owner

I love your books. They have a lovely, chatty style and are easy to read. I especially like the humour - it makes me laugh out loud at times. But most of all they are so informative and have helped me deal with a few issues with my own dog. Thank you.

Carol M, dog owner

CONTENTS

INTRODUCTION

Everyone gets stressed at times. But what is stress? How do you recognise it in your dog? How does your dog experience stress and, most importantly, what can you do about it?

I wrote this book during 2020-2022. The first few weeks of lockdown were oddly calming and I enjoyed the solitude. We walked locally with Gus and the clean air and quiet roads gave us time to enjoy our beautiful countryside and were wonderfully restorative.

But the novelty quickly wore off. I was restless and irritable. Anxiety sometimes overwhelmed me and I battled to find motivation. It was difficult to focus on what I needed to do.

I swung from determination to make the most of the situation to feeling it was all hopeless. I struggled to concentrate. Oddly, my memory seemed to be failing as well. I'd forget to do things, which created even more worry.

I was stressed.

Stress is the body's reaction to feeling threatened or under pressure. Stress can be the result of situations or events, especially where you might have an overwhelming pile of things to do, or where you don't have control over what happens.

This described me to a 'T' - there was an enormous amount of work to do moving Down Dog's training online. We had nearly 1,000 members join our Canine Challenge Facebook group within the first week, so it was clearly filling a need - but I felt the strain of keeping cheerful and thinking of new ideas to share to help people train their dogs at home.

It was tough. One good thing came out of the experience though - I realised just how debilitating it is to have to cope with stress day after day. Which has made me even more sympathetic to the stressed clients and dogs I see.

Stress can often be motivating - it can help you achieve the things you want, and it can help you meet the demands of home, work and family life. A little stress is good for everyone, including children and puppies, to help them develop resilience to cope with the inevitable pressures and strains they'll meet in life.

But too much stress, and ongoing stress, is bad. Constant stress never allows you to return to biological baseline. Harmful or negative stress is felt as distress.

Distress occurs particularly when you don't have any control over situations. Life will always include bad stuff, but having some control can help you (and helps our dogs) to cope and bounce back quickly. Lack of control and frequent unpleasant experiences creates the opposite effect and affects welfare negatively.

Stress and fear can be damaging to us and our dogs, producing mental and physical health problems in people and a rise in stress and reactivity in dogs.

Over-aroused, hyperactive and stressed dogs are those who are easily overexcited, often reactive to other dogs, and are frustrated, worried, scared or anxious. They may find it impossible to relax and calm down and can have a high desire to chase, hunt, sniff or herd. Often labelled 'naughty but nice' dogs, they can also be called aggressive, angry, overconfident, dominant, or even evil.

This book is about how to help dogs who are suffering from problems due to fear and stress. Part 1 explores why dogs feel stress and develop fears. The next chapters describe various common fears in dogs and what to do about them. Then there's a short section all about naughty dogs - those dogs whose behaviour is frustrating, annoying and potentially dangerous - and how to help achieve peace. Part 2 is all about the noises dogs make. We'll look at the various types of nuisance barking and how to address them to achieve the longed for calm and quiet.

I hope it helps you help your dog - and you might just find it helps you, too.

Please note: The illustrative stories in the book are all based on real case studies but names and sometimes sexes have been changed to ensure anonymity. Except for Gus and I.

STRESS AND FEAR

1

WHY DOGS FEEL FEAR AND STRESS

P*epper dug in all four paws. He moved forward one step, then twirled and panicked, darting from one side of the lane to the other, twisting on the lead, trying to get away from the scary monster ahead in the middle of the lane. His owner laughed. Silly dog. It was only an old sack, scrumpled up on the road and flapping in the wind. She waited patiently, chatting away to her flighty dog until he finally plucked up the courage to approach, cautiously, every muscle taut and ready to flee. Once he had had a good sniff he relaxed and the walk continued without further problems.*

Pepper is a greyhound cross owned by my Daughter no 1. He's a sweet, calm dog generally and copes with most things in life very well. But, like all mammals, including us, if he feels fearful he'll react immediately in the face of that perceived danger and try to avoid or escape from it.

The fear response is a normal part of life. It's aimed at keeping the animal alive. Imagine you're a gazelle, grazing in the vast plains of Africa. You hear a noise in the bushes nearby. Your head shoots up and your heart pounds. You worry that the noise is a lion about to attack - so you run away. If you are wrong and the disturbance was just the wind, the worst that happens is you get some unnecessary exercise and lose a little grazing time. But if you ignored that rustle from the bushes, you could end up dead.

Now we are sensible humans who live without predators poised to attack us - but we still feel fear. Like me, perhaps you are more fearful at night. You notice and react more to an odd noise when everything else is quiet. Your heart flutters when you see a strange shape until you realise it's just a deeper shadow. When you can see very little, your imagination conjures all sorts of terrors lurking nearby. And as for the darkness under the bed - well, all sorts of monsters might lurk there. Even when you know it's irrational, you'll still have some odd fears such as these - and still jump into bed from a distance away.

Your body reacts to stress in a number of fascinating ways:

growth and digestion stop, your immune system is put on hold, and tissue repair stops, all in order to prioritise short term survival. Acute stress produces energy, and has an analgesic effect. A little stress improves memory. Beneficial or positive stress is called eustress. It has survival value – if you're prey spotting a lion you get the chance to run away before being eaten.

Stressors come in a variety of types, but one of the most important factors is how long the stress continues. Some stressors can be severe but brief, for example, being in a minor car accident but unhurt, while others can be long-term, such as illness or poverty.

Have you ever glimpsed a strange curvy, serpentine thing on the ground and had a heart pounding moment before you realised it was just a stick? All of us are pre-programmed to react fearfully to certain things. The response is hard wired into our brains. You and I are pre-programmed to be fearful of wriggly, moving things because they could be snakes. And you will react to a wriggly, moving thing, or what could be a wriggly, moving thing, even if you've never seen one.

Fear is a normal response to an actual or perceived threat or situation. But sometimes fears can become excessive and overwhelming. A phobia is an intense and persistent fear, which goes beyond a rational response, that occurs when a human or animal is confronted with something that feels threatening.

Phobias can occur in response to any scary situation. Phobias may result from previous frightening experiences, sometimes from just one overwhelmingly scary event. My best friend has a phobia about spiders after one crawled over her face in bed. She hyperventilates and has to leave a room if she sees even a tiny, harmless house spider on the floor.

I have a phobia of candy-floss. I ate some from a fair in Nottingham many years ago, then later on that night I became very ill with vomiting and fever. As I was being sick, the candy floss remains and stick were lying right beside me. The cause of the illness may or may not have been the candy-floss (and probably wasn't), but now I can't even think of candy-floss without feeling stressed and nauseated - and I retch if I see candy-floss, even in a picture. Daughter no 2 has a phobia of moths and, strangely, elastic bands, although there has never been a particular event that has caused these, to my knowledge. Do you have any specific fears?

Back to fear, stress and dogs.

Fear and stress in dogs are common. These emotions can affect all breeds and all ages. A behavioural study published in 2020 of nearly 14,000 pet dogs in Finland found that over 70% showed behaviours resulting from anxiety and stress and nearly 30% showed fearful behaviours.

That study confirmed with what I've seen in my dog behaviour cases over the years. Things like noise sensitivity, fear of new situations and fear of certain environments, for example fear of slippery surfaces, are common behavioural problems among dogs.

These fears are associated with the dogs' genetics and breed as well as their living environment and lifestyle.

Let's start by thinking about the effects of genetics.

Fear has a strong genetic component. If an animal is fearful, this can be passed down into subsequent generations. A group of researchers in America bred a line of pathologically fearful pointers and found that they bred true, that is, if a fearful dog was bred to another fearful dog then all the offspring were fearful, without exception.

In other words, if fear is part of a dog's genetic make-up then they will be fearful, even with the best upbringing. Puppies are highly influenced by their mother's behaviour, but the fearful pups in the study above remained fearful even when raised by a non-fearful, non-biological mother. Which is one reason why it is so important for anyone breeding dogs to breed for temperament, not just looks.

Fear and anxiety are influenced by many genes; there is no such thing as a simple "fear gene" that is inherited from one generation to the next. Rat experiments showed that if a rat developed or experienced a strong fear, this could be passed down to their offspring and to subsequent generations, even though the new rats had never been exposed to the fear inducing situation. In other words, traumatic experiences can change the way your DNA works and is expressed - and this fallout could be passed on to your offspring.

Noise phobias can be inherited too. Herding breeds are particularly susceptible to noise phobias. When you select for one trait in an animal others come along for the ride. Noise phobia may be one of these, and it's thought this is possibly linked to a herding dog's heightened environmental awareness and sensitivity - these dogs need to be able to spot sheep a couple of mountainsides away, after all.

Breeding choices matter, even without knowing the exact mechanisms of inheritance. The Canine Behavioural Genetics Project is doing research into the genetic basis for a range of behavioural issues affecting dogs, including fear, noise phobia, anxiety, aggression and obsessive-compulsive behaviours. This work should provide us with important knowledge for the future and should help us improve breeding practices to reduce the likelihood of dogs suffering from these debilitating conditions.

But genetics is only half the story.

The particular combinations of genes that you've received from your parents mean that you'll respond with greater or lesser degrees of anxiety to events in your environment. However, the degree to which your life is affected by this inherited predisposition will depend to a very large extent on what you experience in life - how many stressful events you encounter, and their strength, type and duration. Early, significant, and multiple, stressful events can have a major impact on how you cope with future situations.

Which is what happens with dogs too. Dogs learn behaviours through their interactions with people, with other dogs and with the environment they live in. Insufficient and inadequate socialisation of puppies to different situations and new environments in particular has a strong link with these dogs being fearful of new situations in future, especially loud noises, different walking surfaces, such as slippery surfaces, open stairs or metal grilles. Especially if they already have a genetically fearful disposition.

You won't be surprised to learn that there are significant variations in the fearfulness of individual breeds. For example, in the large Finnish study mentioned above, Cairn Terriers were among the most fearful breeds and Chinese Crested Dogs among the least fearful. Welsh Pembroke Corgis expressed a lot of noise sensitivity but little fearfulness of surfaces, whereas the latter was common among Miniature Schnauzers, Chihuahuas and Labradors.

Common fears and phobias in dogs include:

Sound: frequent fear-inducing sounds include thunder, fireworks and gunshots, but some dogs can become phobic about wind and heavy rain too, like my Gus

Vets: dogs don't understand that veterinary visits are in their best interest, and many of the circumstances around these visits, such as feeling sick, pain, blood tests, new locations, strangers, and the presence of other stressed animals, can add to this fear. If the staff are not comfortable with, or don't have time to help, a stressed animal it can compound the problem.

Situational fears: these include separation anxiety, car travel, stairs, reflections and slippy or polished floors

People: most commonly men, children and strangers

We'll look at these in more depth later on in this book and discuss how you can deal with these fears if your dog struggles.

Summary

- The fear response is a normal physiological response
- Fear and stress are common in dogs (and humans)
- Genetics and early experiences affect how a dog deals with fears and stress

In the next chapter we'll look in detail at how stress can affect a dog's development from conception through to adulthood.

2

STRESSED FROM THE START

I was shaking from head to toe. I felt sick and light headed. A passing colleague paused and asked if I was OK. I wasn't. I was working on the children's cancer unit and I'd been giving the children their chemotherapy, an upsetting but necessary task. Each child had had bloods taken to check that it was safe to give these unpleasant drugs. But I realised I had just given one child their drug without checking the results first. Yes I was tired and overworked, but that was no excuse. I told my consultant immediately then rang the lab to wait for the results. Thank goodness the bloods showed it had been safe to give the chemotherapy. But the stress and worry about that incident has never left me. I could have caused the child significant harm and the mistake might even have led to their death.

As you know, I am The Doggy Doctor. I worked as a doctor in general practice and then public health until I took early retirement and turned my dog behaviour hobby into a business. The incident above happened during a paediatric rotation as part of my general practice training. It was one of the most stressful, scary and unpleasant incidents of my life.

What happens when you feel stressed? The effect on your body is to create high levels of glucocorticoids, stress hormones produced by the adrenal gland. In an acute ('fight or flight') situation this rush of glucocorticoids increases blood flow and alertness. It mobilises energy (preparing you to run) and primes the immune system (preparing you for injury).

If the stress is more gradual or chronic, pulses of glucocorticoids are produced which create sustained, elevated levels in your body. This produces the same physiological preparatory response as in an acute situation, but with an even greater magnitude. Long term, excess glucocorticoids can cause a range of health problems, including immunosuppression, muscle atrophy, osteoporosis, insulin resistance, hypertension, depression and insomnia. Urgh. That's why stress can be so dangerous long term.

At medical school we were taught about type A and type B people, two personalities at opposite ends of the scale. Type B people are relaxed, patient, easy-going and tolerant - the sort of people who never let anything much bother them. They tend to be creative and imaginative. Type A people, on the other hand, are competitive, always fighting to get things done, are highly self-critical workaholics, often trying to do two things at once.

The two cardiologists who identified and labelled these behaviour patterns, Friedman & Rosenman, discovered them by accident. The chairs in their waiting room needed reupholstering and the upholsterer noticed they were worn in an unusual way. Their patients had worn out the arms and the edges of the seats because they couldn't sit still for long, getting up and down frequently. This led to them identifying that people with a Type A personality were twice as prone to heart disease and high blood pressure than Type B people.

Personality is what makes each person unique. It's a result of the behaviour and attitudes you develop as a result of the interaction of your genetics, environment and social variables. Dogs, too, have a range of personalities which develop in a similar way.

Let's look at the different stages of a puppy's life and what's important when regarding their future personality and behaviour.

Pregnancy and Birth

Development starts in the womb, the pre-natal (pre-birth) period. Excessive glucocorticoids are damaging to developing foetuses. Rats who suffer stress during pregnancy produce young who are more easily stressed and whose stress hormone levels are slower to return to normal. If a human mother is stressed, anxious or depressed while pregnant, her child is at increased risk for having a range of problems, including emotional problems, behaviour problems and impaired cognitive development. As adults these people are more prone to anxiety and depression. Similar problems can be found in dogs.

Petting and fussing the bitch during pregnancy produces

puppies who are more able to resist physical stress and who are less susceptible to emotional disturbances. In other words, a relaxed mum appears to produce relaxed puppies.

The converse is also true. Pregnant bitches under stress are far more likely to give birth to puppies or kittens that are easily overwhelmed by their environment. These animals start their lives less protected from stress and may be more reactive.

The Early Weeks

During the neonatal period (birth to 13 days old) puppies learn from smells and from touch. From around 13 days to approximately 2½ weeks of age the puppy's sensory and motor systems develop rapidly. Their eyes open, they start to hear things and they become more aware of their surroundings. They react to things happening in their environment and start to explore this amazing world they've arrived in.

Mild stress is vital for normal development and learning. Gentle handling of puppies during this period produces pups who are more resistant to stress, better able to cope with being alone and also learn better later in life. Even if the pups are exposed to something stressful, the calming presence of their mother keeps glucocorticoid levels low.

Having a mother around is vital. Puppies that are separated too early from their mother are at risk of severe problems. Chronic and excessive stress, especially when an animal is young, is particularly harmful. The stress from separation floods their developing brains with glucocorticoids, which affects brain development and effectively teaches them that the whole world is stressful and scary.

This can happen within mere hours of being separated from their mother, and the longer that separation occurs (and so exposure to glucocorticoids continues), the more impact it has on the developing brain. These animals start their lives less protected from stress, and even good socialisation and training may not be effective in helping them to overcome those physical changes in their brains.

Early learning is also a key factor. Puppies will usually copy what their mother does, including being reactive and stressed. For example, if the mother reacts and barks at strangers, the chances are high that the puppies will too.

The Socialisation or Sensitive Period

I once saw a 12 week old singleton pup who had been kept in a stable all his short life. The owner let him out and he ambled out, cautiously explored and sniffed everything, paused to listen to every noise - but he completely ignored his owner and me.

Early human interaction for puppies is essential. All puppies have an inbuilt capacity to connect with humans and lots of good, early experiences will help raise dogs that are friendly and confident. Dogs that have not had the best start in life can often be scared by other dogs or unknown people coming close, or by particular noises, places, or situations.

During this critical sensitive period, the effects of the puppy's environment have a greater influence on future behaviour than at any other time. An individual puppy's behaviour is influenced far more by the early environment than it is by genetics – hence the vital importance of the breeder doing the right things in the early weeks.

Between 2½ and around 13 weeks of age is the critical period for socialisation of dogs to humans, with the most receptive time being around seven weeks old. If puppies have not had any experience of human contact at all by around 14 weeks old, they may remain fearful and distrustful of humans for life. Recently, some research has suggested that the critical period of socialisation may end even sooner in some breeds, such as Border Collies, and there is also considerable individual variability. The key socialisation period to other dogs is between 14 and 49 days – a potential problem in singleton pups.

Puppies develop a fear response from around 5 weeks of age. The first 'fear period' is between 8 and 11 weeks, when fear of something new becomes greater than the puppy's willingness to approach. If puppies have scary experiences during this time, the effects will last a lifetime and often resurface as the pup reaches adulthood. A puppy who is properly socialised in this early critical period is far more likely to grow up to be happy, confident and calm. They will learn new things more easily, be less likely to respond to new things fearfully or aggressively and are more likely to become a good family pet.

By the time puppies reach their new homes the basic foundations of emotionality and future learning have already been established. Puppies raised in less than ideal conditions and who lack a variety of sensory stimulation, such as in puppy farms, will suffer permanent adverse effects, becoming fearful and reactive. This deprivation also affects their future learning and trainability.

This is why puppies from puppy farms or raised in garages or barns are more likely to display problems and why I get so angry at people who churn out puppies for money. It is so unfair on the dog and the future owner. Breeders are responsible for raising stable, confident puppies and new owners must then make sure their puppy gets lots of fun and happy experiences from the moment they bring them home.

The brain of a 16-week-old puppy has exactly the same number of brain cells as a newly born puppy – but it is roughly 10 times larger. This extraordinary increase in size is the result of the number of connections established between the brain cells as a direct result of all the experiences the puppy has in those first critical three to four months of life. Every single thing a puppy sees, hears, feels, smells and tastes, every meeting they have, and every new thing they discover, produces trillions of new brain connections, all vital for their behavioural and communicative development.

The more positive experiences a puppy gets in these critical early weeks, the more accepting they will be of novel things and situations they meet later in life. This is the time they develop learning skills, problem solving skills, communication skills, and coping skills, so they will deal better with the inevitable frustrations and stresses they'll meet later on.

The Juvenile Period

This phase extends from the end of the socialisation period, at around 12-14 weeks, to sexual maturity, which occurs at around 6 -14 months of age, being later in larger breeds. Developmental stages start to vary widely between breeds from this point on.

During this juvenile period, the puppy develops strength and motor skills. Learning ability develops fully – the foundations for learning are established at around four months of age.

It's vital to continue good socialisation during this time. The second fear period, sometimes called the 'fear of situations' period, occurs sometime between 6 and 14 months of age, corresponding to the onset of sexual maturity: so it occurs earlier for small dogs, later for larger ones.

Dogs who have had no problems with certain situations or things may suddenly become fearful of them. Things like certain noises, or places, or dogs, or certain people. One owner I knew, who had carefully raised and socialised her Rottweiler as well as she possibly could, suddenly found her 7 month old puppy refused to go out of her front door. She lived on a main road and the pup had been happily trotting out for four months - until he put the brakes on. The road was busy and lorries from a local quarry regularly trundled past. It was a classic second fear period response, probably as a response to the lorry noise. I gave her advice to chat happily to her dog and give him time - plenty of time - and the problem resolved itself within a week.

Well-socialised dogs will often sail through this stage easily, but it's vital to continue socialisation activities, and support and help your pup, or they may be at risk of becoming permanently traumatised and then require long-term help and support. Stressors such as rehoming, scary situations, or frightening experiences at this time can have long lasting effects.

Adolescence

Adolescence is a tough period for dogs and their owners. This period begins at sexual maturity and ends when the dog reaches social maturity, generally between 18 months and 2-3 years of age, depending on breed. There is a massive increase in brain connections, and the amygdala (the brain area responsible for emotion, impulses and responses to stress) is enlarged.

For dogs, this period is probably equally as important as socialisation. Dogs at this age learn refinement of social skills. Adolescence is also characterised by risk taking, especially in males - there are many similarities with human adolescence. Dogs may start to compete with other dogs in the household for valued things, and territorial behaviours develop, such as barking at passers-by or visitors. Pushy and aggressive behaviours to strangers and other (non-family) dogs often start during this period.

Adolescent dogs show increased independence, curiosity and interest in their environment – it's common for adolescent dogs to surprise their owners by suddenly refusing to come back when called and ignoring all known cues. Dogs may also try to test boundaries – just like human adolescents.

Adolescence is a most trying time – for dogs and for owners. It's a tricky balance to get right – allowing enough freedom but preventing the rehearsal of inappropriate, unwanted behaviours and avoiding too much stress. Which is why I've included a whole chapter on adolescence later in the book.

Owners need a shed-load of patience and have to repeat, repeat and reinforce, all their basic training during this period. It's no surprise adolescence is the most common age for behavioural referrals – and for dogs being surrendered to rescue.

Summary

- A relaxed mum produces relaxed puppies; a stressed mum can produce stressed puppies
- Puppies go through two fear periods where bad experiences can have a big impact
- The amount of glucocorticoid exposure (stress), and the context under which that exposure happens, have strong effects on your dog's behaviour
- Adolescence is as important a time as early socialisation in your dogs emotional development

In the next chapter we'll talk about whether stress is always bad or not, for dogs and for humans. By the way, in case you wanted to know, I'm delighted to report that the chemotherapy was ultimately successful and the child was declared cancer free.

3

HOW DOGS REACT TO STRESS

I *was scared. It was my first try at this. What if no-one was there? Would I get tongue-tied and not be able to speak? Would it be just a huge flop? We were running our first ever Down Dog Live Q ad A session. It's very daunting facing two cameras (we didn't want to take any chances!) a sound recorder, a laptop and an iPad thingy and having to talk to imaginary people you can't see. Luckily I don't have much problem talking.....especially about doggy things. The wonderful Gareth took care of all the techie side, so I just had to manage myself. This required several trips to the loo, lots of deep breaths, and a fixed rictus smile, which relaxed a little once we got started.*

Stress is scary and disabling. Anything new is stressful - a new place, experience, or situation - even when you've chosen to do it.

In the end I enjoyed our first live session. We had been given several questions beforehand and we had a couple more during the broadcast. Once we started, I began to cope. Yes, we got some things wrong. I talked a little too fast (another effect of stress); I was thrown a bit by the laptop showing the stream around 10 seconds later than real time, which is very disconcerting; and we didn't have a good system to monitor the comments people made in real time. But we learnt from our experience.

As do our dogs.

It's your job as an owner to make sure your dog has positive experiences. And if they have a negative experience, you need to take action to try and mitigate and make it more positive for your dog as soon as possible.

A common perception is that stress is bad. Certainly high levels of stress are bad, and so is intense stress, especially when it becomes distress, but a little, low level stress is important for all of us.

Stress is only bad when it reaches a level that is too uncomfortable to tolerate easily, or when it is chronic. And that is what makes assessing stress difficult – each individual tolerates different levels compared to others.

Recognising stress when it affects you negatively is what is important, especially in dogs because your dog can't say to you, as people can, "gosh, this is difficult, I'm struggling here." It's up to you (and your dog trainer) to recognise when your dog is stressed – and to do something about it.

There are many signs of stress in dogs, many of which are similar to those seen in people. Here's a summary of some of the signs you might see when your dog is in a stressful situation, for example, at the vets. Just remember – context is everything!

Air scenting – the dog sniffs in the air towards the "threat", trying to gain information

Avoiding eye contact – the dog won't look you in the eye

Barking or whining– stress barking *sounds* anxious. There's more about this in the later chapters on vocalisations

Loss of bowel control – can include diarrhoea or loose motions

Dilated pupils – the dog needs to take in all the information he can

Ears held back – ears flat back or held back against the head

Ears flushed – red colouring of the inner ear

Furrowed brow, curved eyebrows or **twitching whiskers** – caused by facial tension

Extended (spatulate) tongue – the tongue looks too big for the mouth and hangs out

Curved tongue – the tongue is curved up at the edges from tension

Raspy, dry-sounding panting – nervousness reduces saliva production

Yawning - can be a sign that a dog is tired, but it can also signal stress

Drooling – stress can cause excessive salivation

Lip licking or tongue flicking - dogs lick their lips when nervous just like us

Head turn – the dog will turn their head away from a fear source

'Whale Eye' – the dog turns his head away but keeps looking at the perceived threat, showing the whites of his eyes

Tense jaw – the mouth is closed, and the dog is preparing for action

Low tail carriage, uncertain tail wagging – indicates discomfort and uncertainty

(Brief) Body freezing – the dog is still for a few seconds before reacting or the dog freezes until the threat goes away or he decides to use fight or flight

Shaking – caused by adrenaline release

Digging – especially at floors/floor coverings or anything that's around

Over-activity or pacing – the dog can't stay still (just like us) and this can include tail-chasing, which may be a stress sign in some dogs

Sniffing the ground – possibly to gain information, possibly as a displacement activity

Scratching or checking genitals – again, just like us, especially men...

Sweaty paws – dogs sweat through their foot pads

Paw raising – can be a sign of stress, but always think about the context

Piloerection (hackles raised) – the hair on a dog's neck and spine stands on end (like human goose bumps), making the dog appear bigger while releasing odour from the glands contained in the dog's hair follicles

Penis crowning – dogs may show their "lipstick" when stressed

Urination - some dogs may "leak" when stressed

Most importantly when training dogs: **Lack of focus** – an anxious dog finds learning difficult and they often **won't take treats.**

The rush of adrenaline and glucocorticoids, especially cortisol, that occurs in acute stress can cause other symptoms. This spike of hormones causes raised hackles, which are most often a sign of arousal rather than aggression. Your dog might also show shedding (hair loss) from this blast of chemicals in their body. With most dogs, stress hair shedding is mild. You might notice a bit more loose hair than normal as you fuss the dog, or you might see scurf in the fur. But shedding can be dramatic.

I once saw a rescue dog whose owner was worried about their over-the-top behaviour out and about whenever they saw another dog. We met at their home where the dog seemed fine, friendly but relaxed. We went down to a local beach where there was plenty of room to keep well away from other dogs. The change in the dog was stark. As soon as he saw another dog in the far distance he froze, then started trembling, lunging and barking, and hair flew off him as if he were being groomed. Purely from stress. Poor dog. His road to recovery was long and difficult.

Many of these behaviours and signs can be attributed to other causes besides stress, of course. For example, scratching excessively could be caused by fleas or diet allergies, paw raising can be due to a thorn or cut, and other physical signs by pain or illness. However, once these other possibilities are eliminated, consider whether stress may be the problem.

If stress becomes chronic, your dog may show a further range of problems, such as

1. Excessive itching
2. Digestive problems
3. Housetraining issues
4. Aggression
5. Lethargic behaviour
6. Isolating themselves (hiding)
7. Decrease in appetite, or
8. Destructive behaviour.

Many, perhaps most, of the dogs I see in my behavioural practice are stressed to a greater or lesser extent. Owners are usually stressed too, by their dog's unwanted behaviour.

How dogs respond to fear/stress

What do YOU do when you're scared or frightened?

Consider these scenarios:

- It's the middle of the night. You are jerked awake by a thud from downstairs. Your partner is away from home and you're alone:

Or

- You've stayed up to watch a great film on TV. The house is quiet as you go to bed. You wander into the bathroom, turn on the light and there's a huge hand-sized spider on the wall right by the loo.

What do you do?

Hide in a corner or cupboard? Run screaming out of the house? Ring 999? Grab something to defend yourself with? Stand on a chair and yell? Have a meltdown? Cry?

When something scary happens suddenly, rational thought flies out of the window and a fast and dirty, reactive, lizard-like part of the brain called the amygdala, takes over.

This is your survival brain, which focuses on ensuring your short-term survival to get you out of trouble. There's no sitting down to consider what might be best and weighing the pros and cons in your thinking cerebral cortex, your amygdala just fires up your sympathetic nervous system and your body is flooded with adrenaline and cortisol ready for action.

Heart and respiratory rates increase, pupils widen, sweat glands are activated, mouth goes dry – oh, and the sympathetic nervous system also controls sexual arousal, but we'll not go into that here...

The whole focus is to prepare your body for fight or flight. It's your amygdala that helps you swerve to avoid that oncoming car, or leap out of the way of that falling branch, or jump sideways to avoid that spider (falling over the knickers around your ankles is just an inevitable casualty - why are there so many spiders in bathrooms?)

There are four main survival strategies used by all mammals, commonly known as the Four Fs, and they are usually described in this order:

Flight

Fight

Freeze and

Flirt or Fiddle about

Dogs (and humans) don't just chose and use one of these strategies – they may use one main one or a combination. Previous experience and the success of the chosen strategy will determine which option your dog will choose first. They'll use the one (or ones) that worked well for them before. Things that work are rewarding - and the emotional effect of finding relief from stress is a very strong reinforcer.

Chronic stress

Acute stress occurs in response to stressful events or situations, like our live event foray and the dog on the beach I described above. But chronic stress can be damaging long-term to dogs - and to humans, causing health problems such as gastric ulcers, arrested development, memory problems, immunosuppression and cardiovascular disease.

The stress hormone cortisol is one of several similar compounds called glucocorticoids. Glucocorticoids are a class of steroid that are broadly stress-related. They are linked to physical and emotional stress and play a role in regulating stress responses throughout an animal's life.

The amount of glucocorticoid exposure and the context under which that exposure happens can have strong effects on the behaviour of the individual.

There is some research in abused children that suggests strong negative childhood experiences can literally shape brains, by changing connections and activations so these children constantly feel danger and fear. Traumatic childhood events can lead to mental health and behavioural problems later on in life, especially anger, addiction and even criminal activity. These children become hyper-alert to danger and hypo-alert to the pleasures of everyday life.

It's reasonable to extrapolate these findings to dogs - and it fits with what we already know. Genetic make-up plays a huge part and is probably the most complex bit of the equation as we mentioned earlier. There is a common saying – there are no bad dogs, only bad owners. We like to think we can fix almost anything through good behavioural understanding and training, but the truth is that in-bred emotional states such as fear are a very powerful force.

Puppies born to stressed mothers, or those separated too early, start their lives less protected from stress. The flood of glucocorticoids they experience affects their brain development and effectively teaches them that the whole world is stressful and scary.

Because the brains of these dogs are actually wired differently, socialisation and training protocols may not be as effective in helping these dogs to overcome the physical changes in their brains.

As dogs get older, chronic glucocorticoid exposure can increase aggression—particularly redirected aggression, where the dog turns and bites their owner when faced with a stressful situation.

Effects of stress

Stressors come in a variety of types, but one of the most important factors is how long the stress continues. Some stressors can be severe but short in duration (like when you safely survive a traffic accident), while others can be long-term (such as continuing financial difficulties). These long term stressors are the most dangerous since psychological research has shown that these can cause a variety of physical and mental problems.

People under continuing stress are more likely to have cardiovascular and immune system difficulties and are also more likely to suffer from depression and other psychological problems. The same holds for dogs. In fact, the same types of drug treatments are used to treat stress in both humans and canines. Vets often prescribe the canine version of Prozac for chronic stress and depression in dogs.

But stress is not all bad.

Exposure to stress can be advantageous to brain development and can even improve health outcomes in the long term. It's how much stress you or your dog experience that's important.

Without a little stress, you wouldn't learn anything new, you wouldn't try harder at anything, you wouldn't take any action and you wouldn't progress in your job or career. It could be argued that without stress humankind would never have developed as it has done. Tiny puppies who experience a little, gentle stress grow up to be the most resilient dogs.

As well as how much stress you experience, how well you recover from that stress is also important. An interesting piece of research showed that dogs who had a strong initial physiological response to stress and recovered quickly showed more desirable behaviours (as assessed by owners) than those who recovered slowly.

But even a single, excessive stress can cause problems. Think about members of the armed forces in war zones seeing their colleagues blown up or being badly injured themselves, or an individual in an horrific accident. If the amygdala becomes over-sensitive (such as from trauma after a terrifying event) or over-used (such as from chronic stress) it can fire off too easily and too frequently.

In humans we call these events panic attacks, or in its severest form, post-traumatic stress disorder.

In dogs, we call them behavioural problems.

Summary

- A little stress is good, too much is bad

- Pre-birth, early, and chronic stress and single traumatic events can have long-lasting negative effects
- All dog owners should learn to recognise the signs of stress in their pets

Many behavioural problems arise from stress and its sister state, arousal. We'll look at arousal in more detail in the next chapter.

4

STRESS, AROUSAL AND PERSONALITY

Bobby was a gorgeous Labrador who was refusing to go outside into the garden, with the inevitable unpleasant result in the house. When we first visited, this poor dog was hiding under the table, stressed and shaking, and he didn't want to come out to say hello. He was panting and wide eyed. It was a sad sight to see a dog so stressed. We don't really know why this behaviour of refusing to go out in the garden started. One reason could be that Bobby had a significant scare or shock when outside in the garden. He also had a known back problem, so perhaps he'd had a sharp twinge of pain when moving up to or around the garden – there are steps up to the lawn and that might have precipitated pain. We will never know for sure. The owner had tried bribing him and pulling him out, but nothing had worked.

Shaking is usually related to high emotions, in humans and in dogs. High emotions set up the animal to be ready to respond to potential danger, which is what Bobby was experiencing, resulting in him shaking.

Although shaking doesn't always mean your dog is afraid. Just like us, dogs may shiver when they get too cold – a common problem in thin skinned, thin coated dogs, like my greyhound mix grand-dog, Pepper. Other causes include pain, fear, anxiety, over-excitement and nerves. There's also a rare disease called Addisons disease which can present with the symptom of shaking in the absence of any other factors.

But the commonest reason for shaking or shivering is arousal.

Bobby was struggling. It took a while for him to pluck up the courage to come out from under the table, though when he did he was a lovely, friendly boy. But as soon as anyone went near the door to the garden he started panicking again. His arousal levels were off the scale.

Arousal can be positive or negative. When it is linked to positive emotions we call it over-excitement, when linked to negative emotions we call it stress.

Arousal and stress produces a complex physiological response involving several areas of the brain. Think about a scary situation you've experienced. The fear response originates as an alarm from the locus ceruleus, an area in the brain stem - people who suffer panic attacks are thought to have overactivity in this area. The amygdala recognises this alarm and immediately recalls similar past events – the amygdala is where fear conditioning happens. This has fascinating impacts on other brain areas such as the hippocampus, the main memory storage engine of the brain.

Are some dogs and people more aroused than others?

Think of different people you know, Some are laid back, calm and slow to arouse, others fly off the handle at the slightest thing - a teaspoon being left in a washing up bowl, or clothes not tidied away into the laundry basket. Some dogs will leap up and bark at the slightest noise, while others hardly lift an eyelid if you drop a saucepan next to them.

All mammals have an inbuilt arousal baseline. In dogs, genetics and early upbringing, as well as training and setting habits in puppyhood, all influence their personality, including how easily they can become aroused and stressed.

If you have a near miss in your car, you feel a bit light headed, your heart pounds and you feel shaky and trembly. That's the effect of the sudden adrenaline flood fired up by your amygdala. And you stay more jumpy than usual for quite some time afterwards. If you keep having those near misses, your body can reset to a higher arousal setting meaning you become aroused more quickly and easily until almost anything makes you jumpy and reactive.

If your dog gets over-excited chasing balls, then repeatedly throwing a ball can have this effect. As does allowing your dog to bark frantically out of the window every time somebody or something goes past. Arousal can then becomes generalised, so your dog may start to react to more and more different things in life.

Repeated or chronic stress is bad because the gap between

baseline and the boiling-over threshold narrows with repeated or sustained stress. Over time the baseline resets closer and closer to that threshold, until almost any stimulus will send the dog over the top.

In other words, owners who allow their dog to arouse repeatedly create a dog who will very quickly and easily become "crazy" or "excited" at even minor triggers.

Why is arousal bad for dogs?

When a person or dog reacts they have reached their limit - their arousal threshold. They boil over. They might shout, lash out or even hit someone. It's the same with dogs. Anything that increases arousal moves a dog towards their threshold - the point at which they react. At that point they might start spinning and barking, or lunge at other dogs, or even snarl, snap and bite. You'll find people saying "he barked with no warning" or "the bite came out of nowhere", but this is almost never the case – all the little things that happened in the minutes or hours before added up so that the final, perhaps tiny thing, sent them over threshold.

Let's take the example of a pet dog. They start their day at baseline having rested all night. Their family gets up and greets them - first spike in arousal. Then the dog goes out into the garden to eliminate and sniff around - second arousal spike. Soon after, the owner comes out and throws a ball for them a few times and there's a third arousal spike. After breakfast the owner gets out the harness and lead, ready to take the dog out for a walk. The dog gets excited - the fourth arousal spike. Off they set. Then the dog is surprised by a dog running up to them at the park and boom - this event sends them over threshold and they bark, lunge, and turn into the devil incarnate, much to the surprise of their owner.

We'll talk more about threshold in subsequent chapters, but for now, take note of these two key points about arousal:

- Arousal and stress are cumulative, and
- Full recovery back to baseline takes a long time, from 48 to 72 hours.

You can think of arousal and stress as a bucket. Baseline is when the bucket is empty. Events and stimuli all add to and fill up the dog's bucket. Threshold is when the bucket overflows - so you then need to wait until the bucket is empty to reset back to baseline. And there's only a small drain hole.

Are you the cause of stress?

Are you—or, more particularly, your personality and your lifestyle—stressing out your dog? Recent research has shown that the stress level in dogs mirrors the stress level in their owners.

Dogs are not verbal, so they can't tell us when they are feeling tense and anxious. Researchers have to rely on the visible signs and signals of stress as demonstrated by the body language signs we talked about in the previous chapter, such as how the dog's ears were postured, the activity of the dog's tail, and whether the dog crouched, cowered or moved lethargically. But theses signs can't provide a quantitative measure of just how stressed the dog is.

Dogs under stress secrete the same hormones that humans do. The critical marker for stress is the amount of cortisol that is released into the blood system by the adrenal glands. Some molecules of cortisol in the blood also tend to be incorporated into growing hair—or fur. As the hair grows, it captures an extended picture of the amount of cortisol in the body and can indicate the amount of stress experienced by the individual over longer periods of time. In other words, a strand of hair becomes a sort of stress diary.

A research team from Sweden tested the cortisol in fur and hair samples in 58 Shetland Sheepdogs and Border Collies and their owners. The major finding was that dogs and their owners had similar stress levels—dogs with high levels of continuing stress tended to have owners with similarly high long-term stress levels. Dogs with low extended levels of stress tended to have owners who also seemed to be relatively stress-free.

But this research left an unanswered question: what *causes* this association? The investigators asked the dog owners to fill out several different questionnaires which were designed to give information about the personality of their dogs, their typical behaviours, and their lifestyle.

This showed the dog's personality did not have an influence on the owner's stress level, but the personality of the human member of the pair seemed to be the important factor.

The researchers used a measure of what are called the "Big Five" dimensions of personality: openness, conscientiousness, extraversion, agreeableness, and neuroticism. They found that high scores for openness and conscientiousness increased the dog's stress levels while a high level of neuroticism created a decrease.

Openness is associated with imagination and the willingness to explore new things and enjoyment of new experiences. Since dogs tend to enjoy routine and predictable situations, this could help to explain why dogs are more stressed when their owner is high on this personality dimension.

People high in conscientiousness are well organised and tend to pay attention to detail. They dislike messy things and are bothered when tasks are not finished or done poorly. As we all know, dogs are not bothered by details and tend to be messy. That means that having an owner who puts pressure on the dog to be more 'conscientious' is apt to raise the stress level of both of them.

The big surprise came with the finding that people who score high on neuroticism tended to have dogs with lower stress levels. Neurotic individuals tend to have mood swings, are anxious, and are susceptible to sadness and depression. My initial thought was that this kind of person should stress their dogs, which is the opposite of what the research shows.

Why? Well, humans scoring high on neuroticism can form a strong attachment bond to their dogs, and they also use their dog as a social support. This means they give their dogs more interaction and more physical contact. And a great relationship and bond will reduce stress levels in the dog as well as in the person themselves, which could explain this finding.

In short, the researchers concluded that long-term stress hormone levels are synchronised between dogs and their humans, but it is the dogs who are responding to the stress levels of their owners rather than owners responding to the stress in their dogs.

In other words, if your dog seems stressed, you may want to take a look in the mirror.

And Bobby? Our work with Bobby was aimed at helping him relax, giving him space to make his own decisions, then rewarding them well. By the time we left on that visit he was happily going outside onto the patio and even starting to climb up the first two steps towards the lawn. He continued to gain confidence and was soon wandering into the garden again.

Summary

- Arousal and stress are cumulative
- All the interactions you have with your dog are either arousing or calming
- Aroused and stressed dogs struggle to rest properly and may react excessively to any trigger

Reducing your dogs arousal is important for their health and well-being. In the next chapter we'll look at how to manage stress to help your dog get the best out of life.

5

HOW TO REDUCE STRESS

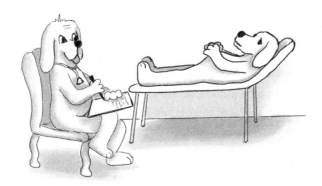

On a canal holiday some years ago we were working down a flight of locks. Experienced by now, we had developed an efficient, effective routine. But in the middle of one flight we were being badly held up by another boat whose lock-working technique was, to say the least, cumbersome and slow. The helmsman wore a captain's cap. He directed his female helper with staccato, barked orders. My mum, a wonderfully kind, tolerant, and gentle person, went to help, but her offer was curtly refused - three times. By the time we reached the penultimate lock there was a considerable queue of boats behind us and several seething crews. Mum could not cope any more and went striding ahead down the towpath, quickly vanishing into the distance. We eventually completed the final lock and sailed on, meeting her thirty minutes later. Her temper had settled and she was back in her usual state of equanimity.

We all have things that annoy us, get under our skin and stress us. For me, it's often when I see unfairness or dishonesty, or when something is done only in a slapdash or incomplete way. For my mum, it's when she can see a better way of doing things and her offer of help is rebuffed. What niggles you?

Life has a habit of throwing bad stuff at all of us. Little niggles can easily build into big stressors.

Some people become fearful and stressed at what seems like something minor to others. My best friend is terrified of spiders and has to leave a room if she sees even a tiny one. She has a full blown panic attack to any spider bigger than a dried pea, after a spider walked over her face in bed one night.

Dogs can suffer excessive fear responses as well - and they can learn fear from having scary experiences.

As discussed earlier, the main causes of fearfulness in dogs are poor breeding and inadequate socialisation. Where and how your dog is bred and raised and what they experience forms their final character and influences how well they communicate both with other dogs and with humans. A well bred puppy who gets a wide range of different, positive experiences from birth is most likely to become a happy, confident, calm adult dog. However, even well bred and well socialised dogs can become anxious and stressed.

Dogs can be become anxious when they are not given enough exercise or stimulation. Physical exercise has been shown to have a positive effect on mood in both dogs and humans - one reason my mum went for her solitary walk when stressed on our canal trip.

Even dogs owned by responsible people such as yourself (well, you've bought this book!) often spend a good part of their lives inside on their own, waiting for you to come home. And when you are home, you're often distracted by everything you need to catch up on after a day at work. Time you spend on electronic devices and watching TV screens takes time away from walking and playing with your dog, which is what they crave after your absence.

The more dogs are engaged in activities and the more varied the experiences and social interactions they have, the less fearful they are in new situations and environments. But there can be an insidious vicious circle with fearful and stressed dogs - you recognise when your dog is fearful or stressed so you avoid putting them in situations that make them feel that way. Which can also make you less inclined, or able, to do any activities or training with your dog.

Lack of control

Sweaty palms, thumping heartbeat, shaking and trembling - all signs of nervousness and fear. Can you remember when you last felt that way? Stressful situations include job interviews, or taking on big new tasks. You'll feel nervous and fearful any time you don't feel fully in control of what is happening or what might happen.

Life will always throw bad stuff at you, but the more control you feel, over the environment, events and possible outcomes, the more you feel able to cope and the more you'll bounce back quickly after disappointments. Lack of control and unpleasant experiences creates the opposite effect.

Control reduces stress. In studies, babies who were able to control a mobile by turning their heads were happier. Rats enjoyed exercising control by turning a light on - even though they didn't like light – simply because they could. Animals who perform behaviours to get a reward are more content. Animals who have control have higher welfare - they are happier.

Where things are uncontrollable, that is, when what you do doesn't change whether something happens or not, that perceived lack of control can lead to apathy, giving up, and may inhibit learning.

The concept of *counter-control* is also important. Counter-control is when an individual responds to an unpleasant situation by trying to gain control for themselves, attempting to control the controller, as it were. For instance, if you punish a dog repeatedly, they will almost certainly fight back at some point. Counter-control can be active (fighting, or running away), or passive (not responding, or showing resistance or withdrawal behaviour), whatever works to change the behaviour of the person doing the controlling.

So how can understanding this help your dog? You can't allow them to wander off and do what they want, surely? No you can't. But you can use your cleverer human brain to give your dog the illusion of control. In other words, you decide which options you offer and then let your dog choose between them.

For example, when I take Gus on our regular morning walk there is a choice of routes we can take, so I let him choose which way he prefers to go. I might offer Gus a choice of rewards and let him choose. These things provide choice and a feeling of control. I can almost see him puff up his chest and walk taller when he makes such choices - they're good for him.

Giving animals (and humans) control, or at least the illusion of control, has many advantages, including reducing fear and improving well-being.

Another important factor which reduces stress is predictability. Predictable effects are soothing whereas unpredictable events can increase stress. Predictability is learned, from the environment or from patterns. When you know and understand what is going to happen, you feel more content and less stressed.

Gus enjoys predictability. First thing, he expects to go for his morning walk, then we attend to the bird table before we have breakfast. He starts to pester for his Dentastix just before the appointed time for that daily evening event, 8pm. Calling him into the utility room predicts a walk, picking up car keys usually predicts a ride in the car, and so on.

What things are predictable in your dog's life - and in your own?

How to reduce stress

You can help your dog relieve stress in many of the same ways you relieve stress for yourself. If you're seeing one or more signs in your dog that they may be stressed or overly anxious, try some of these ideas to get them back to a happier, more playful state.

1) Go for a Walk

That brisk walk helped my mum calm down. The same goes for your dog. A good walk is not only important for their body and physical health, it's good for their mind, too. On a walk, your dog gets to spend quality time with you and burn off some physical and mental energy. A good walk, preferably a sniff walk or the opportunity to run around off lead, is especially important if your dog is inside most of the day, for example, while you are at work.

2) Check the diet

A good diet is essential for good health. You need a balance of protein, fat, carbohydrate, vitamins, and minerals. Are you feeding the right food for your dog based on their size, age, and breed?

Different dogs need different nutrition at different stages of their life. Growing puppies need a high energy, high protein puppy food, old dogs need a food lower in protein but rich in important vitamins and trace elements, for example. Talk to your vet about what diet is right for your dog and if and when you need to change things. But a note of caution here - if you do change foods, make sure you transition gradually, over five days or so, to make it easier on their digestive system.

Also, make sure your dog is getting enough water. Dehydration can cause issues such as irritability that can lead to, or worsen, stress.

3) Provide a quiet den

Perhaps you've noticed that your dog takes themselves off to their bed for a rest when you are pottering around the house. Dogs like the comfort and security of their own bed or den. Make sure your dog has a place they can call their own in a cosy corner away from the busy, high-traffic areas in your home and away from loud music centres, TVs and front doors.

4) Establish a Routine

Dogs, like humans, are creatures of habit - think Gus and his 8pm Dentastix. If you have scheduled times for feeding, walking, playing, and training, your dog will anticipate, know and be prepared for what is going to happen next - they'll feel in control. Having a regular routine is especially helpful when you take your dog to a new environment such as on holiday, or when new animals or people visit or stay at your home.

5) Make time for your dog

You love your dog, but when life gets hectic, your dog can often be the one that sometimes get ignored. Remember that you are your dog's favourite person and you control what happens in their life. All they ask in return for the wonderful affection they give you is some of your attention, everyday. It doesn't matter what form that attention takes - doing some training, playing sniff, fetch or catch games, or just cuddling up to watch TV - your dog will feel calmer, and happier when you make time to focus on them.

Treating stress and fear

Many of the dogs I see in my practice are stressed and need help.

There are two mainstays of treatment for fear and stress. The first is about linking the stressful events or things that cause fear in your dog with something wonderful. For example, you can take your dog to visit the vets without them having any treatment and give them super high value treats there before coming home. And you can act happy and cause your dog's favourite treats to rain from the sky if a car backfires on a walk.

The second is about gradually helping your dog cope better with the fear-inducing thing or event. For example, you can place the nail clippers on a low table and give your dog yummy treats nearby, then pick them up and continue the treat-fest, then bring them closer to your dog while the treats continue, and so on.

These two elements are practically always used together and they have posh dog trainer names:

Counterconditioning is pairing a good thing with a feared thing so that the dog sees the previously feared thing as good. We usually use food for this, as there is good evidence that food helps create new (non-fearful) pathways in the brain. The key point is that the food is given every time the scary things appears – and continues while the scary thing is still around.

Desensitisation is gradually increasing the *intensity* of the feared thing, but only as fast as your dog is able to cope, such as training your dog to be happy about nail clippers. This needs to be done very, very slowly, watching your dog for any signs of stress of fear. Most people try to do this far too fast. Patience is essential as this training can take a long time.

It might be helpful to think of a pair of scales where initially the fear is far too heavy for your dog's ability to cope. When you increase their confidence in coping with whatever is causing the fearful reaction, you start to 'balance' and finally to outweigh the fear.

Although training is crucial in treating fears and stress, a dog that is too panicked or stressed can't learn, so your training won't get very far. You may then need to consider drug treatment. I generally prefer to avoid drugs, for myself or my dog, but if you're at a point where your dog's quality of life is affected, for example, when they are struggling to cope even with the normal things that happen day by day, then adding in drug treatment can be useful.

There has been something of a glut of over the counter "calming medicines" marketed for dogs over the past few years, including herbal treatments such as skullcap and valerian, tablets such as YuCalm or Zylkene, oils or drops such as Bach's rescue remedy, pheromones such as Adaptil and calming treats and chews (nutraceuticals). However, good quality evidence for their benefit in different stress or fear problems is generally lacking - most of the evidence quoted is anecdotal or empirical.

Drugs marketed specifically for canine anxiety include Clomicalm, Trazadone, fluoxetine (Prozac) and Xanax (alprazolam), which are basically meat-flavoured versions of human anti-anxiety and anti-depressant medications. They are not miracle pills and should only be used to support a behaviour change programme under the guidance of a vet working alongside a behaviourist.

Please seek advice from your vet before using any medication. Drugs are not a long term solution. "There's a pill for every ill" is a common myth, for humans and dogs.

I specialise in helping fearful, stressed and reactive dogs in person and online. Our Resetting Reactivity course, available from our online training Academy (online.downdog.co.uk), has been highly successful in helping owners learn the skills to support their dogs to reduce stress, tolerate frustration, learn to control their impulses and keep calm, building their confidence and reducing their reactivity.

In the next part of this book I'll discuss specific fears and stresses in dogs and give you some tips to help you to help your dog cope better and overcome their fears. But please, seek behavioural help as soon as you can if your dog is struggling.

Summary

- Excellent socialisation and a varied, active life can minimise stress in dogs
- Dogs who have a predictable routine are calmer and happier
- There are five simple ways to relieve stress
- Seek help early if your dog is struggling

In the final chapter in this section I'll tell you about the dog that changed my life and we'll examine some common myths around fear, including whether there are bad dogs or only bad owners.

6

BAD DOGS AND OTHER MYTHS

I'd been told about a farmer who had an unwanted litter of collies. The puppies had been shut in a shed for all their lives to that point with very little or no contact with people or the other farm dogs. When I went to see them, the five puppies tumbled out into the sunlight, blinking and uncertain. Warily, they tested out the novel concrete and slowly pottered around. I felt so sorry for them and despite many inner reservations, we brought home Mack. Mack was an apprehensive, fearful dog who was scared of his own shadow. He was suspicious of everything and everybody. He was reluctant to leave the house to go for walks, hated loud noises and sudden movements, and even had to be taught to play. Worse, he snapped at me often and bit me several times, seemingly out of the blue.

Mack was our fourth dog. I'd attended dog training at a local dog club and then become a trainer there for several years by then. I thought I knew a bit about dogs and training them. But I wasn't prepared for this level of problems. Poor Mack. I was out of my depth with him - and scared of him at times. I wept with frustration nearly every day because I didn't understand why he was doing these things or how to help him.

Our vet referred us to a dog behaviourist. Mack spent the hour-long consultation hiding under my chair. The behaviourist's suggestion was "to counter-condition and desensitise EVERYTHING." I vaguely understood what he meant. He didn't show us how to do anything - we just received a written report. We understood we needed to give Mack treats whenever we met or came across anything he seemed scared of, but we didn't understand what should then happen or what to expect. We really needed more practical help, which was not offered - we were left to muddle through by ourselves.

I worked really hard with Mack. We finally got him to tolerate going out for walks and travelling in the car, but we always had to be very careful with handling him. I never let anyone else get too close, as he couldn't cope with new people. He bit me several times and also bit four members of my family. Mack taught me a huge amount in the years before he finally left us. He was the main reason I became The Doggy Doctor.

If you're struggling with your dog, you are not alone. I felt, and still feel to an extent, ashamed by my inability to help Mack become a happy, settled dog. I was embarrassed by other people's reactions, constantly stressed because I worried about him biting someone, and frustrated by the achingly slow, infrequent, and tiny flickers of progress we made. And I felt grief. Grief for the 'normal' dog I wanted to have and wanted him to be.

But he taught me more than I could ever learn from any amount of books and courses. He changed me for the better. I became far more tolerant and patient, which has made me better able to cope with stresses in my own life, as well as in helping other people and their dogs. I can empathise - oh boy how I can empathise - with owners who are struggling with their dogs behaviour. They need as much help, care and support as their dogs.

And when you are struggling with a fearful, stressed dog you can rightly become irritated by the trite comments you can get from other people or might read in books or online.

Fear and stress are emotions. They are not under conscious control and every individual experiences and feels them differently, resulting in a wide variety of physical and mental effects and resulting behaviours. Trying to add labels and using generalisations is not helpful, and there are some common phrases you'll hear that are simply not true.

So in this chapter I want to bust four of the common myths around fear:

1) "There are no bad dogs, only bad owners"

This is a total myth. Yes there are, sadly, 'bad owners', but there are also 'bad dogs'. Hopefully you'll understand by now that poor genetics can produce a 'bad dog', irrespective of the quality of its upbringing by the most dedicated owners.

Poor upbringing by the breeder can create a 'bad dog', even when the genetics are reasonable. Breeders are responsible for setting the good foundations for all subsequent behaviour. If they don't do a good job, they risk creating a 'bad dog'. And new owners who don't continue a good start from the breeder will also be at risk, albeit lower than if breeding and early rearing was poor, of ending up with a 'bad dog'.

Breeders have an enormous responsibility to raise puppies properly and give them plenty of social experiences. New owners need to continue this for at least the first year of life if the pup is to grow into a well-adjusted, happy, confident, sociable pet.

But new owners can only work with the material they get – that's why choosing the right dog in terms of breed, personality, and temperament is so important.

If you want to know more about how to chose the best dog for you and what to look for when selecting a breeder, see our free Pre-Puppy Purchase webinar and accompanying notes on our website at downdog.co.uk. If you live close to us we will even come and help you choose the best pup for you, for free.

I wish I'd had this knowledge when we got Mack.

2) "She's frightened because she's been abused"

How often have you heard an owner say "it's because s/he's a rescue dog" when their pooch develops or shows problem behaviours, especially fear based ones? Or:

"We think she might have been hit by a stick because she runs away from the brush." Or:

"I think he was abused by a man because he's afraid of men."

Many rescue dogs are fearful but it is rarely because they have been abused. We hear these explanations quite a lot, but it's almost always untrue except in a small number, around 1%, of dogs.

The majority of fearful reactions in dogs are not because of any history of abuse, but rather because of a lack of good socialisation. Dogs that end up in rescue have often had a bad start in life. Their genetics may be poor - think puppy farms and the current fad for cross breed dogs with funny names - and the breeder and initial owners, either through ignorance or neglect, didn't make sure the puppy had sufficient experiences of what the dog will meet later in life to set the foundations for confidence and becoming a good family pet.

Perhaps the litter was unwanted. Perhaps the breeder and new owners found they didn't have time to care properly for the dog. Perhaps they just didn't know, or try to learn, what they needed to do to help the puppy grow into a confident adult dog. Perhaps they bought the puppy for their children to cuddle, but once out of the tiny puppy stage they decided they didn't want a gangly, obnoxious teenager. Which is why so many dogs end up in rescue centres. This problem has definitely got worse as society has become more throw-away.

Rescues do a wonderful job. Many dogs find themselves in rescues through no fault of their own or their owners and I'm thankful that the secure safety net of rescues is available. But I am so frustrated by seeing so many rescue dogs who have problems that could easily have been prevented by better early care and training.

I would even argue that not socialising your puppy properly is a form of abuse..... Hmmm.

Let's move on.

3) "You mustn't reassure or cuddle a fearful dog"

Have you heard this one? "You'll just teach them to be more fearful," according to the traditional wisdom.

This myth has been around for ages - that trying to soothe a frightened dog just makes them worse. I suppose it sort of seems logical: your dog hears thunder, he runs to you and you pet him. So hasn't your dog just got reinforced for running to you when it thunders and for being afraid of thunderstorms in the first place?

No, and here's why. No amount of petting is going to make it worthwhile to your dog to feel panicked. Fear is no more fun for dogs than it is for people. The function of fear is to signal to the body that there is danger present, and that the fearful individual had better do something to make the danger, and the fear that accompanies it, go away.

Think of it this way: Imagine you're eating chocolate late at night when you realise someone is trying to break into your house. Would the pleasure of eating chocolate reinforce you for being afraid, so that you'd be more afraid the next time? If anything, things would work in the reverse—you might develop a subconscious discomfort around chocolate. But you're not going to be more afraid if a second burglary occurs because you were eating chocolate the first time it happened.

There's another reason petting your fearful dog doesn't make him worse. Research suggests that petting does not decrease the level of stress (as measured by cortisol levels) in the dog receiving it. But other hormones and neurotransmitters are released and increased when petting, including oxytocin, prolactin and endorphins—all substances that are associated with good feelings and social bonding. So, while petting your dog when they are fearful or stressed may not decrease the associated cortisol levels, it's still possible and indeed likely, that something good could be happening.

Absolutely you should comfort and cuddle your fearful dog – as much as they want. They need to know you are there for them and will help them.

4) You can't catch fear - fear is not contagious

This is an important myth to address. Fear is indeed contagious. One way you can make a fearful dog worse is by being scared yourself. The emotion of fear is so compelling that it is easy to spread around. 'Emotional contagion' is an ethological term used to describe the viral spread of fear within a group, and it's a common occurrence among social species, including humans.

I spent some time as a school doctor, which involved giving mass vaccinations such as tuberculosis and MMR (mumps, measles and rubella) to groups of school children. We were usually set up in a large hall for these sessions. The children were brought in in class or year groups and lined up, waiting. We dreaded a child reacting badly, because if one child screamed or fainted, it was highly likely that the emotions would quickly spread and many others would do the same.

If you're afraid of storms or the dark, it is entirely possible that your dog will pick up on it and become more nervous in those situations. If you are scared of strangers or other dogs approaching, then it's likely your dog will develop those same fears. If you panic at any loud noise, your dog may also react.

However, even if you are scared by certain things (and who isn't sometimes?), all is not lost. You can calm yourself down by concentrating on your body—slowing down your breathing and your movements, changing your posture to one of confidence and relaxation, and speaking slowly and calmly. These actions have the beneficial effect of altering your own emotions - and that will also change how your dog is feeling.

In other words, the calmer you pretend to be, the calmer you'll actually feel.

It's important that you learn how to keep calm yourself if you want to help your dog through any fears they might have.

Can you think of any other myths around stress and fear? Do get in touch and let me know of any and I'll address them in a future edition of this book.

Summary

- Only buy a puppy from an excellent breeder - do your research
- Most fear has its roots in poor socialisation
- Fearful dogs need cuddles and reassurance
- Dealing with your own fears can help your dog, too

In the next section I'll look at some specific problems that have their basis in stress and fear, why these issues might arise, and what you can do about them.

COMMON FEARS IN DOGS

7

HOW DOGS COMMUNICATE FEAR AND STRESS

I *felt eyes on me. I looked up to see Gus staring intently at me. He lifted a paw and placed it gently on my knee. I glanced at the clock. It was 8pm, time for his evening dental chew. Dutifully, for I am a good owner and have been well-trained by my dog, I went to fetch the chew. Gus lay down and chomped happily away for a while, then he stood up, went over to the patio door and scraped at it with his paw. "Do you want to go out?" I asked. He walked towards the back door - yes, he did. Gus can't talk, but he certainly tells me what he wants.*

Dogs can't talk to us, but they can communicate. Dogs communicate with their body and sometimes the sounds they make, which allows you to know what is going on in their little canine heads. Being able to communicate effectively is one of the most important life skills for anyone, dog or human.

Communication is defined as "transferring information to produce greater understanding". We use sounds to communicate with our dogs, talking to them as we do to other humans. We teach our dogs to respond to our words. Training is about helping them understand what those words mean, to allow us to communicate what we want them to do.

Our dogs also learn how to help us understand what they want to communicate. They may run to the door when they want to go out and they easily learn to ring a bell for the same purpose. They will get into your line of sight and stare at you when they want attention or some other specific response. They might nudge your arm or leg with their hard, damp nose, and they will produce a range of different sounds for different communicative purposes.

With dogs who are stressed or fearful, your number one goal is to help your dog be confident. In order to do that, you need to be able to understand how your dog communicates how they are feeling.

I talked about the signs dogs may show when they are stressed in chapter three, but acute fear causes some specific signs. A fearful dog may show some or all of these:

- cowering,
- lip licking,
- panting,
- a furrowed brow,
- moving slowly,
- yawning,
- shaking or trembling,
- not eating, not taking treats,
- unable to settle, scanning the environment (hypervigilance),
- drooling, and
- pacing.

As fear increases dogs may also shed hair, drink and/or urinate excessively, bark, indulge in destructive behaviour, and they may growl and show aggression.

With phobias, all these signs may be present and in addition the dog may eliminate, self-harm and try to hide. One time, Gus was so stressed by hearing gunshots that he tried to dig through the concrete garage floor simply through blind panic. Thankfully, using the techniques in this book, he can now cope well with those unpleasant noises.

A helpful aid to learning how to read what your dog is telling you is to use the acronym TEMP, first promoted by the great, late, Dr Sophia Yin, which I've developed a little further into TEMP(S). It covers seven things you should look for and note. Each of the things I'll mention may not mean much on its own, but when you put them together you can learn to understand what your dog is telling you.

But before we start, one final, crucial, thing to mention - all these signs need to be interpreted depending on where you and the dog are and what you are both doing. Context is everything when interpreting dog behaviour.

Let's look at each element in detail.

T is for Tail

Dogs use their tails for signalling and also for balance. Dogs with docked tails find it more difficult to balance and they aren't able to communicate properly to other dogs, which is one reason I'm glad the practice has generally been banned.

Tail movements are a great indicator of your dog's emotional state, but you must always take the breed into account as different breeds hold their tails naturally in very different ways - think of a Husky versus a whippet. You need to look at the height the tail is held, the amplitude (size) of the wag, and the speed of the wag.

Many people will think "oh the tail's wagging, there's a happy dog". Not necessarily. You've got to look at *how* the dog's tail is wagging. Some dogs will wag their tail and create an entire body wag, or their tail goes round in a circular motion – these are dogs demonstrating delight. My first dog, Ben, always wagged his tail like that when my mum visited.

Perhaps the tail is held very stiffly above the dog's back, which could be the dog being a little territorial, though remember some dogs have a naturally high tail position. Some dogs may tuck their tail in and underneath them and hold it clamped along their belly. They may do this when they're cold, or because they are a whippet, but it is often a sign of anxiety, stress, or a lack of comfort with the situation.

All these different wags and movements can lead to problems if you don't interpret them correctly.

In general:

- a low tail with just the end wagging frantically indicates a lack of confidence or nervousness.

- a slower speed wag means the dog is assessing the situation.

- a friendly, happy, confident dog will wag his whole tail from side to side at a medium speed at mid-height.

When greeting each other, dogs will often hold their tails out straight, wagged from side to side– this means they are slightly tense and ready for action if needed.

When a dog is not quite sure what's happening and is feeling uncertain, you'll see a tail held up or out but fairly still, often pointing towards the left.

An excited and deliriously happy dog will wag his tail all the way round – called a windmill or helicopter tail.

A tail carried high or over the back usually signals arousal. Beware the dog with a high tail where just the end wags fast, almost vibrating – trouble may well ensue.

T is also for Treats

When relaxed and calm, dogs will usually take treats gently and carefully.

As dogs become aroused or stressed they will start to snatch at treats, grabbing at them – a useful sign of stress to monitor in classes or when working one to one with your own dog.

As the arousal or stress increases further, as dogs reach or go over threshold, they may refuse to take treats at all. Try never to reach that point, or, if you do find your dog not taking treats, do something immediately to calm things down.

E is for Eyes

Dogs (and humans) find direct, open staring quite rude and a bit threatening. But staring into another being's eyes can also be a sign of attraction, fascination or adoration. The eyes tell us exactly what the dog is thinking and feeling.

The breed of dog can make a big difference. It's much more difficult to see the eyes properly in very furry breeds, or see them at all in some breeds such as the Hungarian Puli.

Some breeds naturally have fixed stares which don't necessarily mean the dog is thinking about attacking you. The Border Collie is the best example, but there are others too, such as the bull breeds, some terriers and sight hounds amongst others.

Staring is often a sign that a dog is intent on a target. Or perhaps the dog could be looking at something they are nervous about. Context is everything.

Eyes that have an oval shape, a soft gaze, and a liquid, friendly "look" signify a happy, content dog.

A dog with eyes that are moving naturally (like a person who is taking everything in) is a relaxed dog.

A dog whose eyes are darting hither and thither might be a dog who is not comfortable with the situation.

A dog who stares fixedly at something is a dog who has intent on possibly pouncing and playing, or potentially attacking.

Eyes also show if the dog is not being friendly – we call it a 'hard eye'. It's pretty unmissable and makes you feel uncomfortable and get goosebumps. It's how dogs tell you to 'keep away" - and it works well.

Dogs who are friendly and social will generally use soft, 'squinty' eye contact -and they will blink frequently, just like humans do. Rapid blinking is a sign of stress, something I saw Gus do recently when he was very stressed by multiple, loud, car backfires. He also drooled, dropping gollops of saliva all over the car seat - another sign of his stress.

E is also for Ears

Dogs' ears aren't just for hearing – they're also for communicating. The ear position and movement will help you understand what your dog is feeling.

There are huge differences in natural ear positions between (and within) breeds and the muscles in a dog's skull allow them to rotate their ears into many different positions.

When dogs are relaxed or asleep, their ears are held in a neutral position.

Dogs who notice or focus on something, or are attentive to something, will prick their ears, that is, they will pull their ears up and forward.

If your dog's ears flick back and forth they might be listening intently, trying to work out what you're saying, or what that noise outside is, or they may be unsure about what's going on.

Ears that are pinned back can signify that the dog is particularly happy about something – or alternatively, that he is very unhappy about something. You have to look at the whole body language picture and the context to be able to tell.

M is for Mouth

The mouth isn't just for eating, licking or barking – it also gives you an abundance of information about what your dog is feeling.

Mouths can be slightly open, wide open or closed, with the lips loose, or pulled back. The tongue can be hanging out a lot, or a bit, or not at all, or flicking in and out. Perhaps your dog is panting or yawning.

Your dog's mouth when they're relaxed, or approaching in a friendly way, is usually partly open, with the teeth covered and the tongue visible or slightly protruding and lolling. The lips are soft and the dog appears to be smiling.

The shape of the lips is also important. The area at the back part of the lips is called the commissure and it can tell you a lot about the dogs emotional state. A C-shape signifies relaxation and happiness. If the dog is nervous or worried by something, that commissure becomes pulled back, and V-shaped.

Dogs pant when they are too hot. But panting when the dog is not hot is usually a sign of stress. It's one of the things we watch closely for in training classes because it can be an early sign of stress in that situation.

If something attracts a dog's attention, or the dog hears a noise, or alerts to something in the environment, the mouth usually closes and the dog looks alert and focused.

Yawning may well mean the dog is tired – but there can be many other reasons for yawning. Stress can cause yawning. Typically, uncertain or worried dogs do a "shallow" yawn, where their teeth remain hidden. Dogs who feel threatened will do a "wide" yawn, showing all their weaponry – this can be a low-level threat, or it can also show the dog is aroused. Remember, context is everything.

Dogs who yawn during training may be stressed, under pressure, or confused. But dogs may also yawn in happy anticipation.

Lip licks and tongue flicks are often seen with yawning and they can be a sign of stress. But, as always, context is important. If you've just given your dog a tasty treat, you'll see lip licking - but that's not stress, it's because of the yummy taste and the flow of saliva it creates.

You might see your dog's tongue come up over his top lip, especially in photos – many dogs find that strange contraption held in front of their owner's face a bit threatening. That nose lick, where the tongue flicks out over the nose and moistens it, helps the dog collect scent to provide more information about the situation.

Lip licks and flicks can be a sign that your dog is nervous about a person or situation. As stress increases, the dog may lift their lips, showing you their teeth. This may then be accompanied by growling, pinning their ears back, and staring. A nervous dog pulling back and holding their lips tightly against their mouth is a dog showing great discomfort.

P is for Posture

Dogs use their body – where the weight is placed, the posture and the movements – to communicate a lot of information.

Dogs who are nervous or feel threatened will commonly try to make themselves as small as possible, so they lower their bodies and sometimes crouch down. They might crawl and even turn the body sideways with a little frantic body wag. That is a dog who is not confident and might be slightly nervous, saying "I'm not 100% sure about this situation but I really, really would like to experiment with it. Give me time."

Dogs will lean away from any perceived source of danger or from things they find unpleasant – like cameras or looming people - and you will see their facial expression conveying concern.

Confident dogs, or dogs who want to try and avoid a problem by appearing confident, will lean forward and often almost walk on their toes, with their body weight forward, ready for action.

Friendly, relaxed dogs have a centred body weight.

A dog who is stiff, with head up and fixed, and maybe with the hair on the back of the neck, around their shoulders and at the base of their tail standing up, is a dog at, or over, threshold. They may be excited, they may be alarmed, they may be trying to make themselves big to protect themselves, but the dog is alert to something.

A dog with a stiff, upright posture, moving slowly, is a confident dog who is ready to assert himself if needs be.

Remember: context is everything.

S is for Sounds

The final 'S', sounds, may or may not be present in many situations, which is why it's in brackets in our acronym, but sounds can be important when dealing with fearful or stressed dogs.

Dogs can produce an amazing variety of sounds and noises – whines, squeaks, yips, barks, and growls. Each has their own meaning and range from excitement and happiness to fear and intent to defend themselves.

Generally, low-pitched sounds (such as a dog's growl) can indicate threats, anger and the possibility of aggression. These are often interpreted as meaning: "Stay away from me."

High pitched sounds can mean the opposite, the dog perhaps asking to be allowed to come closer or saying they are happy for you to approach. When I met Gareth's dog, Tippi, for the first time after a considerable break due to COVID, she screamed with delight when she saw me, with multiple high pitched yips and yowls.

Whining or whimpering often communicates that the dog is not in emotional balance in some way. They might be fearful, or under stress – or excited or expectant. Whining that rises in pitch and almost ends in a sort of yelp is usually a request or plea for something. Whining that drops in pitch or fades away usually indicates excitement and anticipation.

The louder or more prolonged the sound, the greater the emotion behind it.

Howling is a dog's equivalent of using the phone – it's how the dog communicates with dogs in other territories, even when they are a great distance away. A sing-song howl is used to contact other dogs and means that the dog is curious or happy. A plaintive, mournful howl may signal that the dog is in distress.

Growling is another sound that can be misinterpreted. Growling in play is normal – the growl sounds 'happy', and varies in pitch and volume. Growling as a threat sounds very different: low pitched, constant, gradually increasing in volume and laced with menace, it's pretty unmistakeable.

Growling may be absent if the dog has been told off for growling, something you should never, ever do. When a dog is repeatedly disciplined for growling, the dog will decide not to use their voice, and you don't ever want that to happen. A dog growling is saying "I'm not comfortable with the situation, please take me out of it." This is vital information for your dog to tell you. When you remove the growl from a dog, all that dog has left to try is a bite.

I've written a whole section on vocalisations later in this book and there'll be much more about aggression in dogs in Volume 3 of this Problem Pooch series.

Reading dogs' TEMPS

Ninety-nine percent of the dogs out there will show you these signals in a predictable way. BUT - always remember to look at the big, overall picture, because context is everything.

Dogs can't talk to us, but they can communicate through their face, body and sounds, which allows you to understand what they are feeling and experiencing. Learning how to recognise what your dog is 'saying' to you is something every owner should practice - and the more you practice, the better you'll get at understanding what your dog is telling you.

The worst thing that you can do is not believe what your dog is communicating. Your number one goal is to help your dog be confident by them knowing you will help them out if they start to struggle.

Noticing the signs of stress as early as possible helps you to assist your dog best, to get out of, or cope better with, a difficult situation, and, most importantly, avoid your dog needing to escalate their behaviour.

If you want to know more about this fascinating subject, I've created a whole course on canine communication in my online Academy at online.downdog.co.uk.

Summary

- Learn how to recognise what your dog's body language is telling you
- Take action if you see any signs of stress or fear in your dog
- Ask for professional help if you are struggling

In the next chapter you'll find out about a common problem that is often linked to stress: biting the lead.

8

LEAD BITING

M andy was excited. Her new puppy, Milo, had been given the all clear from the vet after his vaccinations so Mandy could finally take him out for a walk. She clipped her new lead onto Milo's lovely blue collar - the clip was almost as big as Milo's ears - and tried to set off, only to stop suddenly. Instead of walking with her, Milo lay on the floor, trying to bite the lead. "Come on, Milo," she said, fondly, laughing at his silly antics. "We're going for a walk." But Milo planted his bottom on the floor and turned into a devil-dog, snapping and biting at the lead. Because she was bigger and stronger, Mandy finally managed to get Milo out of the house. But the lovely stroll round the neighbourhood she'd planned was a nightmare of refusals, spinning and lead biting. The lovely new lead was bitten nearly in two and there were bite marks and scratches up the whole length.

Poor Mandy and poor Milo. Lead biting is a common problem, and not just in puppies. It's a behaviour that can result from many different causes.

Puppies will bite the lead for two main reasons. Firstly, because they dislike and may be scared by the tension it produces around their neck, like Milo. Understandably, they want the pulling to stop and they don't want to be dragged along. Even if they do walk with you, they want to explore and sniff, not walk in a straight line down a pavement, but when they try to investigate those enticing scents, that pesky lead stops them in their tracks. So they bite, hold onto and chew at the lead.

The second reason puppies bite at the lead is because they want to play and that lead is a novel new thing. These dogs will latch onto the lead, shaking it and growling. When they walk with you they may jump up at the lead to grab it. These dogs see biting the lead as a fun social interaction game - after all, if they grab the lead and pull, their owner pulls back and they have started a fun tug game.

Older dogs may also bite the lead, often for similar reasons to puppies. For others, they have learnt that biting the lead is a way to gain their owner's attention, even if that attention involves shouting and anger: for many dogs, negative attention is better than no attention.

Some dogs may bite the lead from boredom.

Other dogs use biting at the lead as a outlet for pent-up energy from arousal and excitement perhaps due to being overwhelmed by a cornucopia of smells, movements, noises and environmental stimulation, or when they finally go out on a walk after being cooped up alone all day while you are at work. For these dogs, lead biting is a way to release the tension they are feeling.

Frustration is a common reason for lead biting. Perhaps your dog wants to go and play with those dogs over there, but the lead stops him from doing so. That frustration boils over into lead biting.

In fearful or stressed dogs, lead biting may be an avoidance or displacement behaviour - a way of getting you to stop the walk, or to persuade you to go a different way, or to interrupt your training attempts.

What you can do to stop lead biting

When your adorable pet has bitten through several leads, you may decide that enough is enough and want to stop the behaviour. After all, the lovely lady at the local pet shop is starting to look askance at you as you buy yet another lead. Whatever the cause, lead biting is a behaviour that is best stopped early because it can quickly and easily become a habit which can be difficult to break.

Teach puppies about the feel of a lead and collar from the start. Let them drag a house line around the house. A house line is a light, thin line like a lead without a handle. Be careful if using a lead as it can get stuck under doors or around objects. Take your puppy out on lead to their toilet area each time, and start loose lead walking training by practicing walking a few steps at a time with you holding the lead around the house and garden.

If your dog already bites the lead, here are a few ideas to help stop them from destroying more leads in future.

1) Deal with the cause

Work out *why* your dog is biting the lead. If your puppy is frightened by the lead, using it gently for short periods around the house and garden first will help them to accept and enjoy it. One good way is to put your puppy on lead when you take them out to eliminate.

If your dog seems to have too much energy, or appears bored, then give them more exercise and mental stimulation. Make sure you take your dog for a good walk out and about every day - a run in the garden, no matter how many balls they chase, is not a substitute for a good walk with lots of sniffing. Mental work is important, perhaps more so than physical exercise.

The easiest way to increase the mental exercise your dog has is to ditch the food bowl. Why encourage them to scoff their grub in a few seconds when you can use it to work their body and mind over many minutes?

Let them search and forage for their food by laying food trails, playing hide and seek, and feeding through food toys such as Kongs and snuffle mats. Encourage them to work for their food, just as you work for your pay each month, by using it as rewards in training. Play scent games and allow plenty of sniffing on walks - using their nose is hugely tiring for your dog and gives them a great mental work out.

2) Teach your dog to walk on a loose lead

This is by far the best way to prevent or stop lead biting, as well as making walks more pleasant for you and for your dog.

Only about a quarter of dogs receive any regular training. Teaching your puppy or older dog to walk nicely on lead is an important element of all basic training programmes and if done early will usually prevent lead biting from crossing your dog's mind and starting in the first place. Loose lead training will also stop you pulling back or tugging on the lead - which will promote and increase any lead biting behaviour. Don't do that.

Our method of teaching loose lead walking involves fixing the lead against your waist by holding the lead and grabbing your waistband with the same hand. This prevents you pulling back on the lead if your dog does try to pull and avoids the effect of Newton's third law of motion - for every action there is an equal and opposite reaction. Then it's all about rewarding your dog for being by your side and staying by your side when you move off together. It's worth using high value treats at first, given very frequently, every step initially, then gradually dropping the number, type and frequency of treats as your dog gets the hang of walking nicely with you.

If you want to know more about this, our signature Perfect Pet course and our specific Simply Stop Pulling course are both available as self-study courses from our online Training Academy, at online.downdog.co.uk

This training always takes longer than you want it to - dogs all walk faster than humans naturally and it can be difficult for dogs to adjust to your human pace. It's easiest if you start as soon as you get your puppy, but the method works with all dogs - it just needs more practice, time and patience with dogs who have already learnt to pull on, or bite, the lead.

3) Distract your dog

If your dog tries to bite the lead when you are out on a walk, distract them by giving them an alternative game to play. Carry an acceptable tug toy with you and play with that, or play 'find it' games by dropping treats or a toy for your dog to sniff out and find.

Some dogs might just enjoy having something in their mouths when out walking. If their mouth is full, they can't bite the lead. If your dog loves having their mouth full, then try giving them something to carry on your walks. A farmer near us has a collie who always carries a plastic bottle in his mouth when he's herding the sheep. According to the farmer, he won't work unless he has his bottle to carry. It's a harmless quirk but it does generate odd looks from passers-by.

4) Prevent frustration

If your dog gets frustrated when other dogs are playing nearby, then increasing distance should be your first move. Stay further away and play fun games with your dog instead, games such as sniff games, training games, and playing with toys.

It is also useful to teach your dog to have better impulse control. There are many games you can teach to help with this, from rewarding your dog for focusing on you (our eyes on me game) and teaching them that calm behaviour unlocks a world of rewards. For example, teach wait at doorways and gateways, and ensure you ignore whining and barking and reward quiet behaviour instead.

5) Use a tool to help

If your dog is a confirmed lead biter, there are some tools that will help you manage and control the problem while you do the training - tools are not long term solutions.

A piece of PVC pipe around the lead can prevent biting, as can a chain lead, although the latter are heavy and can weigh you and your dog down. But they can be useful in the short term.

Try using a well fitted harness with a back clip - it is far harder for your dog to bite the lead because it's above and behind him. Please avoid harnesses that have a straight bar across the front. It's important that your dog can move their shoulders freely, so a Y shaped front piece is best. However, a harness with only a back clip is not a good option if your dog already pulls on lead, as it will make that behaviour worse. A better harness option is one with a clip on the back and at the front of the chest. These are often called balance harnesses and are used with a double lead (or two leads) to help teach your dog to walk nicely on lead. My preference is for the Perfect Fit harness (other harnesses are available).

Finally, there is something called the two lead method, where you attach two leads to your dog. This method is useful for dogs who bite the lead because they want a tug game with it. When they bite one lead, you simply drop that and pick up the other one. Carry on swapping leads throughout the walk. Eventually the dog might decide it's not worth biting the lead and stop.

Training your dog to walk on a loose lead is by far the best way to stop lead biting behaviour.

~

So what happened to Mandy and Milo?

Mandy sought our help. We showed her how to teach Milo to walk nicely on lead. As a foodie dog, he quickly picked up that if he walked by Mandy's leg and paid attention to her he got lots of yummy treats, and the lead biting stopped.

Summary

- Dogs may bite their lead for many reasons
- Work out why your dog is lead biting and deal with the cause
- Teach your dog to walk nicely on a loose lead

In the next chapter we'll talk about why dogs can be shy or nervous with people and how to help them.

9

SHYNESS AND NERVOUSNESS

teve snapped out of his daydream. Molly was acting oddly. She'd stopped dead and was standing in a strange way, head forward but leaning backwards. Then she spun round and shot behind his legs. He looked up to see a smiling woman bearing down on him, holding a small child by the hand. They weren't looking at him, they were focused on Molly. The child was reaching out a hand towards the dog. "Please keep back," he said, "Molly doesn't like..." But it was too late. An unseemly dance ensued, with Steve trying to keep between Molly and the approaching pair, the child trying to pet Molly, and Molly trying to get away. Steve ended up with the lead wrapped round his legs and nearly fell over.

Dogs act like magnets. Many people appear to believe that they are welcome to loom over every dog they encounter, grabbing at their face and kissing them above their terrified eyes. I often wonder if these same people pat the tummy of every pregnant woman they meet, too.

We talked in the first section about how important it is for breeders to try and breed for good temperament, to avoid any stress in the pregnant bitch and make sure puppies get plenty of early interaction with people, and that the breeder and owner follow a thorough and intensive socialisation programme. These are the best ways to try to ensure that puppies grow up to be confident, well-balanced pets who can cope with what the world throws at them.

But sometimes, genetics create a particularly shy puppy. And the normal bell-curved-shape range of personality also means that some dogs will naturally be at the lower end of confidence. I'll be looking at different types of fear in subsequent chapters, but here I want to focus on how to help a naturally shy or nervous dog.

Unwanted approaches

Too often our pooches are subjected to intrusive, unwanted attention from strangers, just like poor Molly.

When Gus was a puppy, around five months old, we went out for a walk at Kearney, a local coastal village. He already had a good recall so he was off lead. As we walked around the grassy path above a stony beach, two young children went running over to Gus and flung their arms around him before I could get to them. I was horrified - I didn't know the children and had never met the parents, who just looked on fondly.

Luckily, (sensibly) I had done plenty of handling training with Gus, including teaching him that humans do funny things like flinging their arms round and cuddling him. He looked a little bemused, but tolerated the children's attention and we walked on with no problems.

That event could have ended in disaster. Gus might have panicked and struggled and if he was scared enough he might even have bitten - and a young child's face is at dog's teeth level.

Sadly this type of situation is not unusual. When we are out and about training with clients, people, with and without children, have come towards us, looking and talking to the dog we are working with and going to stroke him without even looking at us or the owner, or asking permission.

Why? What on earth makes people do this?

If I tried to pet and cuddle someone's child, I'd probably get arrested.

It's possibly something to do with the fact that some dogs are just so cute, especially puppies and all the doodles and poos that abound these days. I suspect Rottweiler and German Shepherd owners don't always face the same problem.

It's up to you to protect your pup.

Protecting your pup

Keeping dog loving strangers from petting your dog is not for the faint-hearted. I'm sure you were brought up always to be polite to people, but this is the time to be rude.

Here are some suggestions:

1) If you notice people approaching purposefully from a distance away, do a smart about turn and head for the hills. Avoiding trouble is always best where possible.

2) Use the "stop" hand. In our Perfect Pet course we teach owners to use this gesture, similar to a policeman stopping traffic. People appear to have an inbuilt inhibitory response to that movement and it usually stops them in their tracks, which allows you to take control of the situation.

You can then decide what you want to do. If you know your dog will be happy to meet and greet them, then explain that you will bring your pup to them. Then tell them how to touch your pup, "Monty loves being tickled under his chin," or "Lola loves people rubbing her chest." These statements help prevent people putting their hands over your dogs eyes and face which very few dogs appreciate. I had an uncle who greeted child-me on every visit by putting his hands on my head and ruffling my hair. I hated it, and it meant I was not fond of him and disliked his visits.

If you don't want people to interact with your dog, or you know your dog won't be happy being petted by strangers, then just say sorry, you're in a rush, or that your dog is not feeling well - and walk briskly away.

3) If you want, or need, to stop and chat to someone, prevent people being able to get close by teaching your dog to hide behind you, or sit between your legs. Stand or step in front of your dog to provide a physical barrier to prevent unwanted attention.

It is *your* choice whether to allow strangers to pet your dog or not - not theirs.

It's better to be rude than subject your pup to unwanted attention, possibly have them frightened or upset, or become over-excited by it.

Your pup needs to trust you to keep them safe.

4) The wonderful Patricia McConnell suggests this approach to determined pet-petters. "Hi, you look like a dog lover," she suggests

you say, "Would you help us teach Barney (insert your dogs name here) here that people aren't anything to be afraid of?"

The most common responses you'll get are along the lines of: "I'd love to! Dogs love me,"or "I have a special way with dogs," or "Dogs know I'm a dog person."

Your job is then to keep them at a distance from your dog using your body to block their further approach as you say, "I'm so grateful that you clearly are a dog lover and know that getting too close to Barney will just scare him. People who don't know dogs often just barge right up and make things worse. I'm so glad that you know dogs well because you'll know that the best way to help Barney is for you to stand still and allow us to walk right on past." Which you then do.

5) I'd always try the approaches above first, but my final tip is simply - be rude. Glare at the person and say "Keep away. My dog doesn't want a fuss from you." Then walk on briskly.

It's up to you to protect your pup.

Nervousness around novel things

Shy dogs aren't just wary with people they encounter out and about. They are often worried by simple changes in the home. Dogs can be puzzled by, and sometimes be afraid of, new and novel items. They may show one or more of the following behaviours:

- barking at the thing with their weight backwards and ears back
- trying to keep away from it and slinking around it while watching it closely
- approaching cautiously, with their neck stretched out, or
- walking up to it happily to explore it and have a sniff.

Which one does your dog do,?

When you see something unusual or novel, you try to make sense of it by comparing the size, shape and appearance with other things you know and have seen. This helps you decide whether something might be dangerous or if it's probably harmless. So the more things you know about and have seen before, the more likely you are to be able to make a sensible judgment about the thing.

Dogs are the same. The more your dog has seen and pleasurably experienced different places, situations and objects, the more likely they are to be curious and want to explore the new thing.

It may not even be a new thing. Just try moving some furniture about and see how your pup reacts. Most are a bit flummoxed initially, but soon accept the changes. Shy dogs might be very spooked initially and take time to adjust. Most dogs will eventually go up to something new to explore it, given time. And that's the most important message - dogs, like us, need *time* to adjust to new stuff or accept new things.

We recently had some damaged plaster work repaired on a wall in our kitchen sitting area. Our excellent plasterer was here for two days. So that he could access the wall and have space to work, we had to move the furniture around. We pushed the sofa over by three feet, and moved two chairs and a small table to the opposite side of the room, leaving an area empty for the plasterer to work in.

Gus was very put out. He couldn't work out what was going on.

First he hid beside the dining table. Very gradually he poked his head out round the table leg and perused the odd looking area. Then he took one step towards it - then another. Eventually he plucked up enough courage to have a good sniff around, but he clearly wasn't happy. Throughout the two days he kept coming to the kitchen door to check out what was going on, but he didn't want to come in.

Finally the work was finished and we put all the furniture back. As soon as his favourite chair was back in its accustomed position, Gus jumped straight on and settled down, clearly very happy to have things back to normal.

Gus doesn't like change. None of us do. Even small changes can affect your dog significantly. One of our client's dogs refused to go into her lounge after she had bought a new vase for a side table.

Another client's dog baulked when a lamp was moved to a different place in a room.

If your dog reacts like this to something that you've changed in your home, give them time. Move around the area yourself, stand by moved items, sit on new chairs, interact with new items. Praise and reward any curious behaviour from your pup, no matter how tentative.

Most of all, give your dog time to get used to the change. As much time as they need.

Ask for help from a good dog behaviourist if your dogs shyness seems excessive or is not settling with the advice given here.

With our help, Steve became adept at managing people who tried to approach Molly. He also did lots of handling and socialisation training. Molly now happily tolerates people coming close because she knows Steve will protect her from unwanted attention.

Please do the same for your dog.

Summary

- Dogs can be shy because of poor socialisation or because of their innate personality
- Protect your dog from unwanted attention by preventing people coming too close
- Give your shy dog plenty of time to get used to new things

In the next chapter we'll examine why dogs might be fearful of strangers and how you can help them

10

FEAR OF PEOPLE

Mavis *was surprised. Pepe was such a loving pet, enjoying cuddles on her lap and staying close to her all the time. Today her niece and her new husband had arrived for a short visit. Mavis hadn't seen her niece since 'Before Pepe,' when the family had emigrated, three years ago, and she had been looking forward to their stay. When they arrived, Pepe barked furiously at the door as he always did - she didn't mind that, his barking made her feel safer - but she'd expected him to be all over the visitors once they came in. Instead, Pepe continuing barking, darting backwards and forwards and running away into the sitting room. When they finally sat down for a coffee, Pepe crept out from behind the sofa and lay down beside her chair, barking every time one of the visitors moved. Mavis wasn't sure how she was going to cope for the whole week. She had a headache already and her visitors were looking uncomfortable.*

Poor Mavis - and poor Pepe. Pepe was a 2 year old Chihuahua. He'd arrived from a rescue as a six month old puppy. Mavis lived alone in a quiet cul-de-sac and walked Pepe every day round the fields next to her house. He was such a loving dog with her that she never dreamt there would be any problems when her niece and nephew-in-law came to stay.

Pepe had a quiet life and didn't meet many people, just Mavis, her best friend Margo who lived next door (they were known locally as the 'M and Ms'), and various delivery people. Pepe had always barked furiously at the postman, so Mavis shut Pepe in the sitting room whenever a delivery arrived, where he barked madly until they left again. The M and Ms had often laughed about Pepe being such a big guard dog in such a small body.

But it wasn't funny that Pepe was behaving in a similar way to her visiting family.

Why dogs become fearful of strangers

There are a number of reasons why a dog might be afraid of visitors or other strangers. Every dog living with humans has a lot to learn about and to cope with, so perhaps it's no wonder that around 15% of dogs are fearful of strangers.

As you learned in the previous section, some dogs are born fearful - the potential for fearful behaviour can be inherited. Poor breeding and poor early rearing can then exacerbate this tendency. It was impossible to tell if that was a factor with Pepe, as neither Mavis nor the rescue had any details about his earlier life.

Rarely, a dog might have an overwhelmingly scary experience which results in them being afraid of people.

Training methods which involve smacking, yanking and jerking, or other punitive approaches such as spray or rattle cans, can cause a dog to become fearful of people, but that was not the case with Pepe. Mavis had not done any formal training, but she had taught Pepe to sit and give a paw using treats.

But the most common reason for a dog being afraid of unfamiliar people is that they have not been well socialised as a puppy and have missed out on essential early social interactions and experiences.

The critical period for socialisation of puppies to human beings is from 2½ to between 9-13 weeks of age. If puppies don't have experience of humans at all by around 14 weeks old, they usually remain fearful and distrustful of humans for life.

Sadly, it's common for people taking on rescue dogs to declare that their dog must have been abused because they are frightened of men, tall people, people with sticks, people with beards, or angry people. This is very rarely the case – the vast majority of these dogs have simply missed out on the good socialisation experiences they should have had.

Some fascinating recent research has shown that dogs perceive men and women differently. Dogs see women as moving away and men as coming forward, which may be one reason why many dogs are fearful of men but not women. Another reason could be that women do a majority of puppy raising.

All good breeders work hard on this vital element of

socialisation, but there is always much more to do once your puppy comes home with you.

Dogs are very literal creatures. They just see what's in front of them. They don't understand that babies grow into toddlers, then into young children, teenagers, young adults, middle aged adults, then older adults. Instead, they see all the different ages and genders of people as separate, different beings.

Think how differently babies look, smell and sound compared to young children and how toddlers, children, teenagers and elderly people are all different in distinct and contrasting ways. Different people move in diverse ways and at various speeds – they can walk, jog, run, sprint, crawl, skip, hop or limp.

There's all the various adornments people can have, from beards and moustaches to glasses, masks, piercings and face paints; from bags to backpacks; from hats to hoods and helmets; from walking sticks and crutches to wheelchairs, prams, pushchairs and Zimmer frames.

I was out at work for several hours during the day with one of my previous puppies, Bryn, so my mum used to come in each lunchtime to let him out to eliminate and have a play time. One day it was raining quite hard so she came into the house with her anorak hood up – and Bryn backed away from her, barking madly. The hood made her outline look completely different and he was scared by this strange-looking creature. Mind you, he was very sheepish once she pushed her hood back and he realised who it was.

There is also the multitude of appearances – those with different skin colours, varying hairstyles, shy, quiet people and loud confident people, tall people and short people, thin people and fat people, people wearing skirts and dresses and those who wear trousers and suits, as well as coats, ponchos, shawls, scarves, earmuffs and mittens.

People vocalise in a huge range of ways, too – whispering, deep or booming voices, high pitched shrieks, sneezing, snoring, coughing, yelling, angry outbursts, laughing, crying - the list is almost endless.

What a lot our dogs have to cope with.

How you can help a fearful dog

Living with a dog that is fearful of people can be difficult. But there is a lot you can do to help them.

The first step to helping a fearful dog is learning to recognise the signs of fear in your dog. Re-read the earlier chapter (chapter 7) on this and practice reading your dog's TEMP(s).

Dogs who are scared of strangers will show many obvious signs, including cowering, lip licking, panting, furrowed brow, slow movement, yawning, shaking/trembling and pacing. Most fearful dogs will move away from or withdraw from a stranger, although sometimes a nervous or unsure dog might jump up at the person. This type of jumping up is like a pushy punch and can unbalance you if you are not ready for it. The dog's aim is exactly that - to push people away and increase distance. Some fearful dogs will try to keep people at a distance by barking at them, which can look and sound very aggressive, as these dogs will often dart forwards to bark, and then scoot back.

If your dog is very fearful it is a good idea to talk to your vet as he or she can discuss if medication may be warranted. Drug therapy can be particularly useful to support the early stages of your training, but it will not solve the problem. Only training can do that. Please ask for help from a good dog trainer or behaviourist if you need.

Your motto for helping your people-fearful dog is to be like a boy scout - be prepared.

Home visitors

Here are some things you can do to help your dog cope better with visitors to your home.

1) Create a place of safety

Some dogs with severe fear may need to go to a comfortable place in your home away from any visitors where they can rest and not have to encounter any strangers. This is often the best option when you have workmen in the home, during deliveries, or when there is more than one visitor that might overwhelm your dog.

Safe spots for dogs do not need to be a large space; a corner of a comfortable, quiet room where your dog can curl up with their favourite toy or blanket is fine. A crate makes a perfect place for your dog to escape to when things get too much.

There are other things you can try - wrapping your dog in a close fitting garment such as a thunder shirt or modified stretch T-shirt, or spraying calming doggy pheromones in their safe spot may help.

Keep them safe from disturbance. When your dog is in their safe spot, do not allow people to go in there. This must be an area where your dog can be left alone and unbothered.

2) Prepare your visitor(s)

Whenever anyone new comes to visit, tell them what to expect beforehand. Ask them to completely ignore the dog. They should not make eye contact with the dog and must not try to pet the dog, no matter how cute the dog is. Of course as soon as you tell someone not to do something, that becomes all they can think of. Be prepared - be ready to talk to them so they can focus on you, or ask them to look at a picture or object nearby, or give them a book or magazine to look at. Anything to stop them looking at your fearful dog.

It is your dog who should get to decide whether to approach a visitor or not, not the visitor. Some dogs may quickly warm to a stranger and allow petting and handling. Alternatively it may need several visits to get your dog used to a new person.

3) Use treats

Teaching your dog to be less fearful is a long process. It involves pairing a good thing with a feared thing so that the dog sees the previously feared thing as good. We usually use food for this, because food helps create new (non-fearful) neural pathways in the brain.

You need to give the food whenever the scary visitor appears and continue to give treats the whole time the scary visitor is still around - this is a great way to give your dog their dinner.

You might hear or read a suggestion that you should give your visitor some treats so that they can drop them for your dog. This is poor advice, because it puts the dog in a conflict situation - they might want the treats but not want to go near the person. Instead, *you* should reward your dog well with treats when they are calm in the presence of your visitor and allow your dog to decide whether they want to approach your visitor or not.

4) Practice produces progress

If you have frequent visitors, you should make a plan to help your dog learn to be more comfortable with them. Try to invite someone round three or four times a week and use the ideas above to help your dog learn that visitors are not as scary as they first thought.

If your dog does decide to approach your visitor, the person should continue to avoid eye contact and make slow, non-threatening movements. Your dog will probably start by sniffing the visitor. Then they might jump up to sniff more. They will go towards then move away from the visitor.

Once your dog spends some time near the visitor, and you can tell that they appear comfortable and calm, the visitor can start to look at and talk to the dog. Perhaps try a tickle under the chin, or a chest rub. This can take a considerable time and must not be rushed. Remember it is your dog who should decide on whether or not they want to interact with the visitor, and for how long.

Never force your dog to accept handling by a stranger, especially a child. If dogs are pushed too far out of their comfort zone and can't get away, they may resort to biting. It's your job to make sure that everyone stays safe around your dog.

Helping your dog out and about

Here are some tips to help dogs who are scared of strangers when out and about. A key first step is to identify what type of people the dog is fearful of - the triggers for the behaviour. It might be all strangers and unfamiliar people or perhaps just some groups in particular such as men, children, people wearing hats, or people walking with sticks.

1) Doggy decompression

The first step is to limit your dog's exposure to their triggers. This might mean keeping your dog at home for a few days to allow them to lower their stress levels and fully relax. Engage your dog's brain by using food games and doing some training to keep them occupied.

Then make a plan to help to teach your dog to cope better. Plan where and when you can walk to see a few of their triggers but not too many. Plan to walk with a family member or friend so they act as a helper to keep people from coming too close while you're training.

2) Teach your dog that scary things are OK

Start off with the triggers at a good distance, the point where your dog can see them but will not react. As with the visitor training above, the key part of this training is to link the appearance of a scary person with yummy food.

The food should start every time, as soon as the scary person appears and continue until they have gone past. Your aim is for your dog to remain calm and non-reacting at all times.

This process will help your dog gradually to change their emotional response from one of fear to one of acceptance.

3) Deal with problems

When training out and about, unexpected things will happen. Someone will suddenly appear from a doorway, or a gaggle of screaming children will run down the road. Have a plan to deal with these situations.

Your two best friends here are time and distance. Turn around smartly and move away when something unexpected happens or your dog starts to react. Then stop and reassess. Can you wait there and train or do you need to move further away? Repeat as necessary.

Severe fear of strangers can lead to aggressive behaviour, including growling, snapping, and biting. If your dog is very fearful please work with a good dog trainer or behaviourist to come up with a plan to deal with your dog's fear. Don't risk a bite. You can always contact me for help. But please do something - being fearful all the time is unpleasant and can damage your dog's health.

Mavis asked for urgent help from me. She followed my advice about helping Pepe learn to be comfortable around her visitors, by giving him space and lots of yummy treats when her niece and nephew-in-law were present. Over the following few days Pepe started to relax and by the end of the first week he was firm friends with the visitors.

Summary

- Fear of people is usually due to poor socialisation
- Give your dog time and space and never force them to interact with anyone
- Use the methods described above to help your fearful dog become more relaxed and comfortable around people

- Seek help from a good behaviourist if you need and especially if your dog is showing any aggression

Many people-fearful dogs will also dislike busy, noisy places. In the next chapter we'll examine why dogs might be fearful of certain places and what to do about it.

11

FEAR IN BUSY PLACES

I t was chaos. Mandy was tired of the village fete. Her two children were getting tired and crotchety and were bickering constantly as they came down from their ice cream and candy floss sugar high. Her husband, Mike, had wandered off to look for the fifth time around the vintage car display, and, to make things worse, Bonzo had started digging his paws in and lying down. He was panting and drooling - perhaps he was as hot, bothered and fed up as she was. She had promised the children they could take Bonzo into the dog show but at this rate they wouldn't get there. Moving thirty kilos of recalcitrant Labrador was beyond her. She just wanted to go home and sit in the garden with a long, cool drink and she suspected that was what Bonzo wanted too.

One of the reasons you got a family dog may well have been the enticing thought of happy family outings - to the pub, the cafe, the beach, the village fete, or forest parks. What could be nicer than enjoying a warm weather wander in congenial surroundings with everyone tucking in to good food and drink and your dog being admired and petted?

Maybe you have a bombproof party animal dog who loves everyone and likes nothing more than all the busyness, noise, and goings-on at your local summer fete. Good for you.

Then again, maybe your dog is like most dogs, and finds traipsing round a hot and busy fairground, on a short lead, with children screaming, people laughing, food smells, loudspeakers blaring constantly and squashed chips in the grass you won't let them eat, a complete nightmare.

You can't put them back in the car as it's far too hot. Your unhappy dog is stuck with this for as long as you choose to stay. Not nice for any of you.

Bonzo was a normally outgoing, friendly, happy-go-lucky dog who loved nothing more than to make new friends when they met people out and about. But he acted very differently at the fete. He stood quietly beside Mandy while the children went on rides, lagged behind her as they moved through the crowds and, to

Mandy's amazement, he didn't even try to eat the crisps her children dropped. Perhaps he was tired.

You may be surprised when your friendly, happy dog finds a busy outing a bit too much. Continually restraining your dog from jumping all over a thousand new friends they believe *must* want to meet them, will wear both you and your dog out. Or perhaps your dog tries to employ their usually effective tactic of barking and lunging so you, the embarrassed owner, drag them away. But when there's nowhere to go to get away from the constant noise and hustle, your dog can easily become overwhelmed.

When things are too much for you, you shut down. You become subdued, stay quiet, and make yourself small. You try not to be noticed, and dread being spoken to, or challenged. You know you're stuck there and you can't change the situation, so you quietly give up. This state is called learned helplessness - and your dog can suffer in exactly the same way. When they can't handle the stimulation of hordes of people, children, other dogs, noises and constant movement, they shut down.

If your dog is the type to prefer their own company, or at most just have a couple of friends round for an intimate dinner party, it might be best to leave them at home rather than over-challenge them on a busy outing. They will be much happier there, snoozing away until you return.

If your dog loves people and enjoys busy places but becomes overstimulated and difficult to manage, then aim to teach them how to be relaxed and stay calmer in those more stimulating environments.

How to help your dog

If you want to be able to take your dog with you to busy places, or you're planning on visiting a big event, there are several things you can do to prepare your dog to cope with these situations. Forward planning is vital when you have a dog. Your dream of fun family and doggy outings might have to be put on hold until you've trained and helped your dog to cope with any situations they find difficult.

Please don't plunge your dog into a new and strange environment where they might struggle, without doing some ground work. You want to be sure they will not only cope, but enjoy the experience. Heading off on busy family outings can only be done safely and pleasantly when you know there's a good chance that, with all your preparatory training, your dog will enjoy it too.

Here's what to do:

1) Find out how your dog copes in busy places

You could start with a short walk past the local shops in the middle of the day, or try hanging around at the far end of the school road at school-start-time or school-coming-out time. (Male readers, please be careful about following this advice. I don't want people getting the wrong idea.)

Other good places to hang out are shopping centre car parks. Start at quieter times of day, then try a busier time, working up to a Saturday.

Some dogs will be much happier out of the main thoroughfares. They'll cope better on the sidelines, where they can safely observe what's in front of them without having to worry about what might be approaching from behind. Standing with your back to a wall, hedge or other barrier will help your dog feel safe from things approaching suddenly from behind them.

Watch your dog closely. Revise chapter 7 on how dogs communicate fear and stress and learn to spot any signs of uncertainty or fear in your dog. If you see any, move your dog away to give them more space. Go as far away as you need so they can become, and remain, relaxed - this might be much further than you think.

2) Recognise any limitations - for you and for your dog

Perhaps you have a social dog who's ebullient, boisterous, and loves everyone. That's great, but it's wrong to inflict that on a pub full of people wanting a peaceful refreshment stop, or to impose a furry mugger on people happily wandering about their own business.

Teach your dog proper manners around people before taking them out to busy places. Our online Perfect Pet course (see online. downdog.co.uk) shows you how to do this if you need help.

Maybe your dog is quiet, shy, or anxious. These dogs might struggle to be in the same space as unfamiliar people and - worse - their strange dogs. Taking these dogs to a busy fair would be their worst nightmare.

You need to be able to recognise your dog's likes and dislikes and the situations they can and can't cope with. Once you know these, you can develop your plans accordingly. Don't assume everything will be fine. Test different situations with your dog and make sure they can cope, and are coping well, before spending any time there.

Here are some ideas:

- Start small. Have a walk with a friend and their dog. Stop for a coffee in a quiet spot.
- Take a trip to your local park. Watch children playing and groups chatting from a distance. Gradually get closer, watching your dog for any signs of stress or excitement as you approach.
- Go out with a group - your family, or some friends.
- Try a pub garden or a crowded beach.

Always be prepared to leave early if your dog is uncomfortable.

3) Teach settle

Many clients have found this skill to be a boon - at home, when friends visit, in cafes, on trains, on buses, at training class, on holiday, at the shops, at friends' houses, at the vet's - the list is endless.

A dog that will settle down quietly when out and about can

come with you to see friends and to visit dog-friendly places and establishments and is a pleasure to take out anywhere. Here is how to teach it:

- Start at home with your dog on a lead. Sit in a chair. You can ask your dog either to sit or, preferably, lie down, or just let them decide a position to be in by your side. You can use a comfy mat for them if you wish.
- Put your foot on the lead around eighteen inches to two feet (45-60cm) from where it is clipped to their collar or harness to prevent them having too much freedom. You want to give your dog enough leeway to allow them to move to change position, but not enough to jump up at you or move any distance away from you. At this point you can add the cue "settle" if you want.
- Ignore your dog. Reward any relaxed behaviour by placing a food reward in front of them so they do not have to move to reach it. It doesn't matter what position the dog is in, sitting, standing up or lying down, and it doesn't matter if they move from the position they started in - they must just be calm and relaxed. Continue to reward your dog fairly often initially, then gradually reduce the frequency of treats.
- At the end of the session (minimum 10 minutes, or the duration of a favourite TV programme), say "that'll do, good settle" or some similar release cue, praise your dog well and take off the lead.
- Once the dog understands the exercise, giving them a filled Kong or favourite chew toy will reward the behaviour and encourage a calm settle.

Practice settle wherever you want the dog to relax calmly – the kitchen, sitting room, home office, and so on. Once your dog has got the exercise off pat, you can practice out and about, for example, while sitting on a bench watching the world go by, while chatting with friends you meet up with, or in dog friendly pubs or cafes.

Settle may be all you need for your excitable, friendly dog.

But you also need to make life as easy as possible for your shy, worried dog.

4) Help your shy dog

Helping shy, nervous dogs means working on techniques and strategies to help them cope in our crazy, noisy, busy world.

Read chapter 9 on shy, nervous dogs again and follow that advice. If you go to a crowded place and your dog surprises you by being 'fine' with all the busyness, remember it's more likely that your dog is finding it overwhelming, so they shut down and wait for it all to be over.

To help your shy, nervous dog, stick to these three key rules:

- Avoid forcing your dog to go to places where you know they will be stressed and unhappy. Leave them at home with a filled Kong or other chews and a comfortable bed to snooze away the time.
- Gradually get them used to meeting up with small groups of friends or family. Take things at your dog's pace.
- Prevent unwanted attention from other people. Use a 'stop' hand, stand in front of your dog, or move briskly away.

5) Forward planning

Be a scout - be prepared!

When thinking of an outing, plan for potential problems and plan to help your dog enjoy it as much as you will.

Take plenty of water - panting, sniffing and excitement mean your dog will probably need to drink more regularly. A cooling mat is a good idea on hot days. When stopping to watch events, try to find an area with some shade. Remember dogs have to wear their fur coat all the time. If it's going to be hot, or you're planning to be out for a long time in the sun, it's probably best to leave your dog at home - heatstroke is potentially fatal.

Take a towel to dry your dog if there might be any rain.

And, of course, take plenty of treats and poo bags.

Plan trips at quieter times where possible - go earlier or later rather than at the peak times. This is especially important on hot days - aim to take advantage of the cooler hours and avoid the midday sun.

An important part of your plan is about being prepared to abort the trip if things aren't going well. If your dog is stressed it's not going to be much fun for any of you. Plan to get out of the stressful place, by going to a quieter area and seeing if your dog calms down. If it is still too much for your dog, cut the outing short, go back to the car and go home.

Equally, if your dog is having an exciting time, with lots of movement, meeting people and sniffing, make sure you factor in plenty of downtime to help them cool, calm and relax before the trip home. Offer them a drink, frequently. Take them for a quiet wander away from the noise and bustle, or find a quiet spot to sit and relax until your dog has calmed down before going home.

Mandy and her young family adored their trips out and wanted Bonzo to enjoy them too. She took Bonzo to several different places to check how he coped and made sure he was the epitome of politeness when meeting other people and their dogs. She taught him settle, planned better for their outings by following the guidance I've outlined, and they had no further problems. With Bonzo at any rate. I don't know about the children.

Summary

- Be prepared before setting out to any event or outing to a busy or novel place
- Do any training you need to do well before any busy outing or trip
- Plan your trip, including your exit strategy, and
- Enjoy the outings you were so looking forward to when you decided to get a dog to share your life.

When planning an outing, you will probably go in your car. But what if your dog is fearful of car travel? That's what we'll look at in the next chapter.

12

FEAR OF CAR TRAVEL

I had our new puppy, Gus, in a cardboard box on my knee. He looked around, puzzled and slightly apprehensive, for the first few minutes of the ride home. Then he started drooling and looking unhappy. Before long, he was sick. We stopped for me to clean up the box, Gus, my jeans and my jumper. Setting off again, after a short while, we experienced the same scenario. Three more times before we arrived home. Poor Gus. And my jeans were never the same again.

Car sickness is common in puppies and young dogs, just as it is more prevalent in children than in adults. Many puppies will be sick at first. Often, the first experience a pup has of car travel is when they are being taken away from everything they've known in life, their breeder, their mum and their siblings. That's stressful.

The three main causes of car sickness in puppies are stress, motion sickness and excitement. The ear structures responsible for balance in young puppies are not fully developed, so they can suffer more from the unusual, odd movements of being in a car. Some pups may find the journey exciting and over-stimulating with new smells, the novelty of moving at speed and seeing so many things passing by quickly.

Conditioning can play a part too, if your dog associates car travel with sickness. When I worked on a children's cancer ward, it was heart-breaking to see some children start to retch and be sick even before the cancer drugs were given, because previous experience had taught them that they would be sick as the powerful drugs trickled into their tiny bodies. It's the same with pups. If, like Gus, your puppy was sick the first time or so travelling in a car, then they will quickly start to associate car travel with feeling, and being, sick.

It's not helped either by the first few journeys a pup takes often being stressful - being taken away from their mother and littermates and visiting the vet to be poked, prodded and have needles stuck in.

Signs of car sickness include:

- Inactivity - your pup might freeze or cower in a ball when they get in the car
- Yawning
- Whining, crying
- Licking or smacking their lips
- Excessive drooling and
- Vomiting

Many pups quickly grow out of car sickness as their ear balance mechanisms mature, but others may not. Of my dogs, two, who had travelled in a car with their breeder from being tiny pups, were fine and never suffered from car sickness. The others all had it to a greater or lesser extent. Some were fine after the first few journeys, including Gus, one took around four months to settle, but one of my dogs, Bill, really struggled.

When Bill was around six months old, we needed to travel three to four hours up to my parents home where we were spending Christmas. There was no way Bill (or I) was going to cope with that, so we consulted our vet for help. He recommended and prescribed a sedative.

I gave Bill the recommended dose the agreed hour prior to travel, but ten minutes later he was sick. I was pretty sure he had vomited up the tablet - so I gave him another one.

I spent the whole journey to my parents on the back seat with Bill almost comatose, terrified he would stop breathing and that I might have killed him. When we arrived at my parents, he reeled out of the car as if drunk, staggered into the garden, peed, and then slept for fourteen hours. Thankfully he had no ill effects the next day and we had a wonderful Christmas break. I gave him the proper dose before our journey home during which he sat up and looked around quite contentedly - and, happily, he was never car sick again.

How to help a car sick puppy

I do not recommend overdosing as a way to help your dog. Instead, here are a few ideas to help your car sick pup.

- Encourage them to face forward, rather than look out of the side windows.
- You could use a car crate, which has the added benefit of containing any vomit, and cover the sides so the pup can only see forward
- Place your pup in the middle of the back seat. They can see forward out of the front window and being in the centre of the car is the most stable place with the least movement, which may also help.
- Open the windows a little while you are moving to equalise the air pressure
- Keep your car cool and well ventilated, as a warm, stuffy atmosphere makes car sickness more likely and can worsen any existing nausea
- Don't feed your pup for a few hours prior to your journey. Some people recommend giving your dog a tiny sugary snack just before the journey as there is some evidence that can help reduce car sickness. Ginger has also been said to help, so you could try a tiny bit of ginger biscuit.

These tips will help the majority of dogs, but there is a small minority who continue to suffer car sickness. These dogs may need more help in the form of tablets from your vet. They may prescribe antihistamines or anti-nausea drugs. There are one or two over the counter medications you can buy that may be suitable, but please never give your dog any tablet without checking with your vet first, as doses may vary substantially from those given for children.

The good news is that tablets may solve the problem in short term, and, once you have broken the link between car travel and being sick, in the long term as well, like with Bill.

But what if your pup or your older dog clearly hates the car or is refusing to even get in?

Does your dog run and hide when you pick up the car keys? Or become a lump of lead, refusing to move towards the car? Do you have to engage in an unseemly chase game to grab hold of your dog in order to bundle them into the car? Then have to hold them there while you do a St Vitus' dance trying to shut the door?

Good breeders will take puppies out in the car from a very early age, but for the any pups who don't get this exposure, their first journeys are terrifying - the movement, noise, strangers, and being taken away from everything they've ever known in life can be traumatic. Or perhaps your rescue dog has never been taken out in a car and you're trying to get them used to it. Some dogs may have once been fine in the car but a traumatic event of some sort, such as a road traffic accident, leads to them not wanting to travel in the car.

Dogs who hate car travel and the car can be a shock for owners. Having a dog who won't travel in a car is very limiting when trying to socialise your pup, stops you going for more interesting and varied walks later on and can severely limit your social and family life.

How to help a dog who hates the car

Helping your pup or older dog learn to be comfortable and settled in your car can take some time. I've described the process below, but please do contact a good dog behaviourist to get more individual help if needed.

It's important that your pup has sufficient room when in the car, to sit or lie down and move between positions when they need. Think about where you want your dog to travel. If you have several family members then your dog may need to travel in the boot. Many modern cars have sloping backs and although there is plenty of boot floor space, the tailgate, when shut, may not give your dog room to sit up comfortably and this may feel claustrophobic to your pooch.

If you have a choice, then consider a crate or car harness so your dog can travel on the back seat. This has an advantage in that there is less movement in the centre of the car, so it may help with car sickness. Plus your dog can see all round and you can talk to and give treats to your dog if needed, more easily. I don't recommend the footwell for regular travel - dogs can easily overheat there, it can be difficult for them to get fresh, cooling air, and they cannot see out.

All dogs travelling in a car should be restrained in some way - there are a frightening number of dogs injured from being thrown around the cabin of a car, and a dog is a heavy missile that can injure human passengers badly if they are loose and you have an accident. It is illegal not to have your dog restrained in the body of a car. Your dog may travel happily unrestrained in the boot, but if your dog travels inside the main area of the car, they should either be in a crate (itself tethered down) or in a car harness and seat belt.

1) Start with a break

Before you start this training process, give your dog (and yourself) a one or two week break from any car travel. Walk them locally or leave them at home. If your dog has had bad car experiences and if it is possible, change the vehicle they have travelled in previously, either to another car if you have one, or some people have even decided to buy a new car. At the very least, change where your dog will travel in your car.

2) Acclimatisation

Then start your training process. This will take as long as it takes, often several sessions over a few days at each stage. Never push or force your dog to the next stage before they show they are ready. Slow and steady wins the race. Repeated short five or ten minute sessions each day are best, rather than one long session.

Start by getting them to see the car as a fun place to be. Start at whatever distance from the car your dog is comfortable and gradually move nearer as your dog relaxes. Go out and play with their favourite toy near the car, feed them yummy treats by the car, sit next to the car and give them their favourite fuss, cuddles and scratches.

Encourage, but do not force, your dog to get in the car. Open the door and sit in it yourself. Have some yummy treats and reward your dog every time they make a move towards the car or put a paw up into or onto the car. Wait until they either jump in themselves, or ask you to help them get in. Leave all the doors open at this stage.

Once they are in the car, reward them heavily. Give them their dinner while they are in the car, feed yummy treats, fuss, play with a favourite toy. The point at this stage if to build a strong association of "car = fun" in your dog's mind.

3) Preparation for travel

During these next training stages, repeat each one until your dog is content and happy. Do not rush this training.

Start to shut the door or boot. You may need to do this in stages - reach for the door/boot, move it slightly, then a bit more, and so on, until you can close it and your dog hardly notices.

Sit with your dog in the car with the windows and other doors open. Gradually shut each door and window, making sure your dog is comfortable each time you progress. Remember, take your time over this training and watch your dog closely for any signs of stress.

Start the engine, then turn it off. Gradually extend the time the engine is running up to a minute.

4) Driving off

Reaching this stage can take a long time. You are probably grateful to have reached this stage and eager to drive off with your pup. But again take this very slowly.

Start moving - but not far at all. Drive or reverse the car down your drive and come back again. Gradually - very gradually - increase the distance you drive, perhaps to the end of your road and back, then, if your dog copes well, you can go further and further.

Once you can drive a short way, try to end each journey somewhere fun - the beach, the park, or a favourite friend or family members's house. Have a short walk and a play before coming back home.

More than anything, be patient. This training takes time. You need to build your dog's confidence and help them to be comfortable and happy in the car.

With Gus we followed exactly this process. He soon decided car travel was A Good Thing and now he adores going in the car, tries to jump in at every opportunity (including trying to jump in visitors cars and delivery vans if he gets the chance) and is most put out if we drive off and leave him at home.

Summary

- Early car sickness is common but most dogs naturally grow out of it
- Traumatic events can cause a fear of car travel
- Overcoming fear of car travel takes considerable time and needs frequent, tiny training steps

Even if you don't need or want to travel much in a car, your dog still needs to be comfortable around traffic. Our roads are all now so busy, you can find life very difficult if you have a dog who is scared of traffic. We'll look at how to help such dogs in the next chapter.

13

FEAR OF TRAFFIC

Doug, the owner of Ricco, an 8 month old collie cross, was very frustrated. He'd had Ricco from when the pup was 8-9 weeks old. Doug had done all the right things, making sure Ricco was well socialised with all sorts of different people right from the start and taking Ricco out to different places and situations every week. Things had been going well. Ricco had seemed happy to go out to different places and see many different things, though Doug had noticed that he had been slightly reluctant to walk near busy roads. Around 6 weeks previously things had taken a turn for the worse. Ricco had been startled by a large tractor coming up fast behind him. Ricco pulled Doug to the side of the road and shot straight into the hedge. Doug had found it difficult to persuade him to come out and walk again, but eventually Ricco came out and they continued their walk. Ricco was not happy - his tail was clamped between his legs and he looked scared. Since that incident, Doug had found it difficult to walk Ricco. Ricco would get in the car happily enough, but when they arrived at any venue with traffic around, he refused point blank to get out of the car, cowering in the boot. If Doug did manage to get him out, Ricco tried to hide under anything and everything as they walked. Poor Ricco and poor Doug. This wasn't what he imagined owning a dog would be like.

It's no fun if walks are unpleasant and scary. Neither owner nor dog gets any enjoyment out of it. We expect our dogs to cope with so much in our busy, chaotic, noisy human world. And most rise to the challenge brilliantly.

But some dogs find it difficult to cope with traffic, especially large, noisy vehicles. Traffic noise can be very unpleasant to us as well as to dogs. Some breeds are more prone than others to be noise sensitive, collies being one. Gus is, though I blame his huge, erect, satellite dish ears for a lot of that. Speed of movement of traffic can also scare some dogs - sight hounds can be particularly prone to that - and traffic movement can trigger the chase and herd instincts in some dogs. And any breed can be frightened by the splashing, whooshing, hissing noises of traffic in wet weather.

Some dogs will cope with cars and other small vehicles, but can't cope so well with large, heavy vehicles like tractors and lorries. Or your dog might cope with intermittent traffic on country lanes, but struggle when faced with busy town centre roads or bypasses. Dogs may cope with traffic approaching them from the front, but battle if traffic comes up behind them.

Dogs can be fearful of traffic if they don't have enough good, pleasant experiences of traffic right from the start - which is why giving your puppy thorough, good socialisation to everything they might meet in life is so important.

But even with well socialised dogs, one scary event, like Ricco and the tractor, can mean your dog becomes scared of the possibility of another similar thing happening again. Worse, the fear often generalises, as in Ricco's case, to all other traffic.

You may find that your puppy was initially quite happy with all sorts of traffic. Perhaps you patted yourself on the back for doing such an amazing job. But at around 7-9 months old, your pup suddenly became scared of cars, or lorries, or bicycles, or any other sort of moving vehicle. It's more common than you might think - many dogs will develop odd fears around that age, which links to the second fear period mentioned in an earlier chapter. A scary event then, such as a car zooming past too close, too fast, may give you a long-lasting problem. Luckily, most pups will get over these fears fairly easily if previous socialisation has been good.

When Gus was young. I walked him along a busy road where there was only a pavement on one side. On the way out he walked normally as he was facing all the cars coming towards him. Then we turned back and he started to panic about any cars coming up fast from behind him, spinning round and flattening himself against the wall that bordered the path. To this day, when he's not happy with noisy traffic approaching from behind, especially vans, tractors, or vehicles with a rattling trailer, he'll flatten himself on the verge until they have passed. I usually manage to anticipate this by spotting any early signs he's becoming uncomfortable and taking him quickly to the side of the road. I'll chat happily and feed him some treats until the problem vehicle has gone past when all will be well again.

Some dogs may only react to certain types of traffic, like Gus. Different breeds will react in their specific ways. Your collie may try to chase cyclists, your Jack Russell may mutter at motorcycles, or your German Shepherd may lunge at lorries. Fear often plays a large part, but remember, fear doesn't always make dogs cower away - they might also lunge forward, in an attempt to chase the scary thing away.

Dogs who react in fear or aggression to traffic can be a danger to themselves and others. Your dog may pull you into the path of an oncoming vehicle, or into a roadside ditch; they may become so het up they turn and bite you; they may cause an accident by running at a passing vehicle that has to take evasive action; or cause pedestrian injuries by lunging across the pavement in front of a passing granny, or child on a bike.

On Saturday recently there was a huge commotion on a road near us. A dog ran out in front of one of the many posses of cyclists who roam our roads every weekend, and the resultant avoiding action by the lead cyclist caused a pile up of several bodies and bikes. One man was badly injured, requiring the air ambulance to attend and take him to hospital, and several others had more minor injuries. The dog was not hurt.

Helping your traffic fearful dog

There is a lot you can do to help your traffic scared dog, but it can take time. You'll need to repeat this training many times over many days. Don't rush things.

1) Avoid busy places and choose your walk times

While you work on helping your dog cope better, it's important to try to avoid places where you know there is traffic that might be scary for your pooch.

Try to avoid busy roads, or roads where the odds are high you will meet a large lorry - those squealing, rasping, huffing, air brake noises scare me, never mind my dog.

Stick to quiet country lanes, parks, woods or beaches where you are less likely to meet traffic. Though it's not guaranteed. One day on the beach Gus and I were chased off because of two quad bikes repeatedly racing up and down. But normally such places are quieter.

Time matters, too. The lane near our house where I frequently walk is normally quiet, but between 7.30 and 8am it's a bit of a rat run for commuters. We meet three times as many cars then than at other times of the day.

And if your chosen venue proves too busy on the day - there's a car boot sale locally, or the fields bordering your chosen route are being cut or harvested - you can always go home or try again later.

Once your dog has gained back a little confidence, start your training.

2) Identify places to practice

Find somewhere where you and your dog can see and hear traffic, but at whatever distance you need for your dog to remain calm and relaxed. This distance may be far greater than you first thought, so you need plenty of space. Locally, for example, we have a beach car park next to a grassy sand dune area which is set back from a not-too-busy main road by a wide pavement, which is ideal. There is room to move further away if or when needed and plenty of opportunity to do the training.

When you've found your ideal spot, settle yourselves down and start training. You should be static at this stage, standing, sitting or perching somewhere, not trying to walk around.

Every time a vehicle passes, chat away happily to your dog and give them plenty of treats. "Oh look there's a lovely red car. And it's followed by that grey SUV, both driving nice and slowly. But here comes a motorbike, slaloming past the other cars, revving his engine to show off his big...bike. Silly boy racer, isn't he?" And so on.

Watch your dog carefully for any signs of stress - revise the TEMP information from chapter seven. If you see any stress signs, move further away. If your dog is relaxed, perfect. Keep training. The aim is that your dog stays relaxed when any traffic goes past, and preferably also has a waggy tail and is enjoying the training.

Once your dog is remaining relaxed no matter what vehicle goes past, it's time to move closer, by around two paces at the most, and repeat the standing-still training, rewarding every time a vehicle passes. Once your dog is happy and relaxed there, move forward another two paces and so on. Move further away again immediately if you start to see any stress changes in your dog.

3) Add movement

Eventually you will find you're standing quite near the road and your dog remains relaxed. Then it's time to add some movement, by walking back and forth for two or three steps to start helping your dog cope when traffic is coming towards you from different directions, in front or from behind. Keep up the chat and frequent treats. Gradually increase the number of steps you take in each direction.

Your dog is your barometer. Whenever you see any signs of stress, do something to reduce it - move further away, stop, stand still and watch traffic go by for a while, or even go home.

Finally, after many more sessions, you will be able to walk your dog proudly along the pavement and your dog will remain calm and relaxed. But the training has not finished at that point, oh no. Now you need to repeat this training in many different locations, gradually finding busier and noisier places to repeat this training.

Training very rarely goes smoothly, so you will need contingency plans. If something scary happens, it's important to keep exposing your dog to the scary thing, but only at a distance and level where he can cope well. Sometimes planning where to go can cause you a migraine, but it is worth a little short term pain to help your dog.

Be patient and remember that practice produces progress.

～

For Ricco, we followed exactly this process. We started with Doug sitting with Ricco at places where Ricco could see and hear traffic, but from quite far away. We did this until Ricco showed he was happy and coping well, then gradually moved closer and closer. Then we practised at busier and busier and noisier and noisier places.

There were setbacks - a refuse truck with very noisy air brakes, clanking mechanism, and reversing beeps caused a small setback, as did a convoy of twelve motorbikes one day. You can expect set backs like these - life happens.

It took a few months, but now, Doug and Ricco can once again have fun walks together.

Summary

- Traffic noise, size and movement can all be stressful for dogs
- Dog who are fearful of traffic can be a danger to themselves and others
- Help your dog relax near traffic by only working at the pace they can cope well with

These last few chapters have covered the common fears dogs might have when out and about. But our modern lives mean that sometimes your dog can't come with you and needs to be left at home. In the next chapter we'll look at another common fear - dogs who struggle with being left alone, why that might be and what to do about it.

14

FEAR OF BEING LEFT ALONE

L ilo hated being left alone. She would run away when her owners tried to encourage her into the kitchen, so they would have to chase after her and pick her up to be able to shut her in. As soon as the owners left, Lilo jumped excessively at the kitchen door, work surfaces and the table, crying and whining. She scratched at and chewed the kitchen door, chairs and table. She paced around constantly and was unable to settle at all. When her owners returned, Lilo's face and feet were all wet, there were puddles of drool on the floor and her greetings were totally over the top. Poor Lilo hated being apart from her family.

Lilo had separation anxiety, which is the doggy equivalent of a panic attack - a dread of being left alone. Separation problems are distressing for both the owner and the dog. Dogs with this problem show exaggerated signs of anxiety when they don't have access to their owners, whether because the owner is out of the home, or even when the owner is in another part of the house and the dog is stopped from reaching them.

If your dog struggles with being apart from you, they can't control their panicky reaction.

Imagine you're in your car. You start to pull away as the traffic lights turn green when a car appears from the side, blaring its horn. You slam on the brakes and manage to miss a collision by just an inch. Your heart rate soars, you hold the steering wheel in a grip of iron, you're gasping and gulping, you feel shaky and sweaty, and a little light-headed.

At the moment you saw the other car, could you have willed yourself to be calm? Could you have told yourself to get a grip and relax? No.

The physiological process of the brain flooding the body with adrenaline in an emergency fear response is involuntary. That's exactly what dogs with separation anxiety are going through when left alone. They can't give themselves a good talking to and persuade themselves to be calm. They are in the grip of their physiology and emotions.

It's a fairly common problem – around 14-17% of dogs are affected. There are no appreciable differences between male and female dogs, but mixed breeds, rescue dogs and the companion breeds are slightly more likely to suffer from the problem, although there is no evidence of a genetic component.

Multiple instances of re-homing – or sometimes just one - can trigger separation problems. Other contributing factors include the dog suffering from a severe illness or malnutrition during puppyhood, if the puppy was the only one in a litter, or if the puppy was removed from the litter too young.

But the most important triggers are human factors. It's common to see separation related problems in dogs when owners have been at home for maternity leave, or after they take an extended vacation. Perhaps you have had to return to work after time off to care for your new dog, but you haven't thought to train your pup to be comfortable being left alone. Other factors include moving to a new home, after a kennel stay, if there are altered social relationships such as a new baby, a new pet, or a death in the family, or any other traumatic event.

Although rare, a medical or cognitive problem, such as seizures or dementia, can trigger or present as separation problems - always ask your vet to check your pet if you see any odd behaviour in a previously content dog.

During the coronavirus pandemic lockdowns, many dogs thought Christmas had come early. They were accustomed to months or years of being left at home all day, alone. Suddenly, their humans were present all day. The lockdowns worried me and other behaviourists because we knew we were going to see many more cases of separation problems as life started to return to normal. Sadly, that has proved to be the case.

There are certain signs that flag your dog is unhappy with being separated from you.

Perhaps your dog is over-attached to you.

Perhaps your dog lies beside you as you tap away on your

computer and they curl up by your feet under the desk.

Perhaps you allow them to sleep in your bedroom (or even your bed).

Perhaps your dog follows you everywhere you go, so you can't even have a wee in peace.

Perhaps your dog gets under your feet as you prepare to leave the house, then they try to push through the door with you.

All these things suggest a separation problem.

In milder cases your dog might pace about, whining, barking intermittently and chewing objects when you are out. But your dog will eat when left alone and is able to settle for short periods. Increasingly we are labelling these cases as separation distress, as there is no evidence of significant anxiety.

Most cases I see fall into the moderate category. These dogs often shadow their owners' every move, even when going to the bathroom. They will commonly not eat treats when left alone; pacing, barking and whining are more constant, and any chewing and destruction is worse and focused on points of entry to their confinement area, such as doors or windows. You might also see sweaty paw marks, panting, and your dog might involuntarily produce eliminations. The excessive greetings when you return may last for several minutes. Lilo was in this category.

Severe cases are thankfully rare. These dogs can bite themselves, especially the front paws and legs or the tail tip or base. They may also do significant damage to themselves and to your home trying to escape - broken teeth and nails and even cuts and lacerations to their paws. They may shed hair excessively. Some have uncontrollable diarrhoea and may not be able to maintain a normal weight.

Is it separation anxiety?

It's important to make sure what you're seeing is indeed separation anxiety. For example, barking excessively may be due to several other causes, or lack of crate or house training can lead to the dog making messes when left.

The cases that are most commonly misinterpreted by owners are where dogs are under-stimulated or under-exercised – the owner returns to a house turned upside down and assumes it is a separation problem. Most of these dogs are just bored and need more work to do. We'll discuss this in the next section of the book.

Owners of dogs who have true separation problems often focus on trying to stop the symptoms - but you need to deal with the problem itself, not the symptoms. We had one case where the owners had nailed plywood over the doors and blocked access to certain areas - but their dog was still highly upset when they went out. Focusing on stopping the barking, or howling, or preventing any damage or destruction doesn't help the underlying problem.

Preventing separation problems

Here are three tips to prevent separation problems. All puppies should be taught to be left alone at times from the day you bring them home. These three tips will also help if your dog is already struggling a little when left alone.

Tip 1: Give your dog some alone time every day

If you're at home all day, this may mean you going out to do some outside maintenance or gardening, or anything else outside while your dog stays in the house.

Perhaps you can take a short trip out in the car without your dog, or take a short walk alone, leaving him in the house. Whatever suits you and your circumstances.

Tip 2: Prevent your dog shadowing you

Shut the toilet door to stop your dog following you in. Close other doors, such as the kitchen door when you're making meals, or shut your dog outside while you're in the house (if safe).

You could use barriers such as baby gates, or use a crate for your dog for short periods, or put your dog in a puppy pen for half an hour. Anything that prevents your dog following you round all the time is good.

Tip 3: Encourage your dog to rest and get enough sleep.

Dogs generally sleep for between 12 and 16 hours a day, which means giving them regular quiet times to relax and snooze, at least a couple of times each day. Set them up to snooze in a comfy bed a short distance away from you, such as in a covered crate, or even better, in a separate room.

But what if your dog already gets distressed when you leave them? Helping dogs with separation problems is a welfare issue - vital for their own mental health (and yours). Please seek professional behaviour help sooner rather than later.

The good news is that around 75% of dogs can be cured and the rest can be helped to cope better. Just remember:

- It's not personal – your dog isn't trying to spite you. They can't control their anxiety.
- Logic doesn't apply – just because you know you are coming back, your dog doesn't. And they will never "get over it" if you don't do anything, in fact, most dogs get worse.
- Punishing your dog is pointless – it will only make things worse. They can't help their reactions.
- Changing behaviour is a slow and gradual process but it does yield results if you stick to your plan.

Seven Steps to help dogs with separation anxiety

Here's the most important thing to know. Helping your dog will take time – often a long time. There aren't any overnight fixes, nor is there a magic wand you can wave. You have to do the work.

The steps I've given you below are a summary of our successful programme for helping dogs with separation problems, but please ask for behavioural help, particularly if your dog has symptoms suggesting they fall into the moderate or severe category. If your dog has only mild symptoms, here are some ways to try to help them, but, I repeat, please seek professional help if you are struggling.

STEP 1: Set a routine

Think about how much of the day your dog has contact with you in an average 'normal' week (if you have one). Be as specific as possible. Identify the regular or usual times you'll leave your dog alone. Or, if your routine is very varied, set some times to leave your dog on their own that you will be able to maintain. You can plan all your outdoor tasks for those times – shopping, gardening etc. If weekends are very different, set out a typical weekend day as well.

Notice how closely your dog stays to you throughout the day. Perhaps you can't even go to the loo in peace, or your dog only sleeps if touching you in some way.

Gus is with me a lot of the time. He stays with me in my study in the day and moves with me to the sitting room in an evening. He sleeps downstairs in his bed in my study or on the settee in the sitting room. He's left alone for part of each day and is happy to be left for 3-4 hours. When I first go out and leave him, he sometimes barks a couple of times or gives a whine or two, but then he settles down and goes to sleep until we get back.

STEP 2: Preventing shadowing

If your dog usually follows you, how can you stop them doing it all the time? Follow the steps given in Tip 2 above - shut doors to prevent your dog following you into every room or joining in every activity with you. Shut your dog outside in the garden for a few minutes at a time while you stay in the house, as long as your garden is secure.

Baby gates are especially useful during this training as they prevent your dog being close to you but they can still see, hear and smell you. As you go about your various tasks you'll naturally move into and out of sight, giving your dog plenty of practice at tiny periods being alone.

STEP 3: Find out what your dog does when left alone

Perhaps your dog isn't happy when left alone. Perhaps you've found your dog has started pacing round, getting under your feet as you prepare to leave the house, then trying to push with you through the door as you try to walk out. They signal their hurt at being left behind by barking, or howling, or shaking and shivering – or even indulging in drooling, eliminations or some wanton destruction.

What does your dog do? You need to find out.

Set up your phone, iPad or tablet with a good view of the room where you'll leave your dog, or the room where they'll spend most time when you're out.

Go out and leave your dog alone for 20 minutes – you need to either drive away or walk away somewhere out of sight. Monitor and record your dog's behaviour during your absence. If you want to watch what's going on in 'real time' you can download an app such as the Alfred app, if you have another suitable device and understand technology enough to set it up.

Please don't follow this step if you already know for sure that your dog already suffers from separation stress. And if you see any significant signs of stress while following this step, please return to your dog immediately.

STEP 4: Teach relaxation

Many dogs need help to learn how to relax. Teach your dog to lie calmly on a comfy bed or fluffy mat, or in a crate, or whatever suits. The area you choose must be comfortable and quiet and the space must allow your dog to lie down and stretch out if they want.

Choose a suitable place as their relaxation spot - somewhere you don't usually sit and relax, such as a not-too-busy hallway, or a less frequented room, such as a utility room or conservatory, or a bedroom. It needs to be somewhere the dog is used to and is happy to be in.

A couple of short sessions a day say three or four times a week will help your dog learn best. There's evidence that both humans and dogs learn best through fewer sessions, more spaced out.

STEP 5: Reduce over-attachment

One of the things that raises the likelihood of your dog developing separation problems is when your dog becomes too attached to one person. Therefore, one way to help prevent problems is to make sure everyone in the household takes turns to interact with your dog.

Of course this might not be possible if you're on your own. In that case, work hard on the 'go to bed and relax' exercise above and make sure you're giving your dog a wide variety of activities. Ideas include:

- varying what games you play, such as tug, retrieve, and food games,
- training your dog to do fun tricks (our Canine Challenge Facebook group has plenty of ideas),
- doing some scent work at home and on walks, and
- playing mind stimulation games (see the free help sheet on our website)

If your dog is already over-attached to you, focus on the ideas in step 2 to help your dog learn to cope better when they are not always with you.

STEP 6: Desensitise departure cues

One of the things that can foster anxiety in your dog is when they learn to recognise your departure cues – that is, the things and routines you do when you are going to leave the house. And boy, they learn these so easily and quickly. Your dog has little to do each day except watch you – so it's not really surprising that they learn our routines almost better than we do.

We all have routines. What do you do when you get up on the morning? Have a shower? When do you clean your teeth? Before or after getting dressed? I guarantee you do the same things in the same order day after day – because it's one of your routines.

So you'll need to teach your dog that certain 'going out' cues don't really mean anything. This is good preventive training but is also essential if your dog shows any signs of separation anxiety. Just imagine the anxiety spike a separation-hating dog feels when they hear or see the first cue that their owner is going to leave them. So it's vital to teach your dog that the anxiety-provoking cues they see or hear are really meaningless.

Think about all the things you do when you get ready to go out. For example, Gus appears by our side whenever he hears Himself (my husband) turn off his iPad after breakfast. That's because turning off the iPad is the first step in the routine of us getting ready to go out and take Gus for a walk. The second step is Himself saying "Right, then", the third step is walking towards the utility room – and so on.

Everybody will have different routines and do different things, but there are some common ones: picking up car and/or house keys, going to the outdoor coat cupboard or wherever else you keep your coats, putting certain shoes on, or packing and picking up briefcases or bags. You may have others to add to this list.

Teaching your dog these things don't matter is all about making these trigger actions less important and taking away any fear or anxiety attached to them. We call this process desensitisation.

Here are some ideas for how to desensitise common triggers:

• Pick up and carry your keys around the house with you, occasionally shake them or rattle them.

• Put your coat/shoes on, walk round, walk to the door, return, take them off

• Fetch your briefcase or bag, walk towards the door, turn and come back and put the briefcase or bag down or away

One key trigger is the door you use to leave through, usually the front door. It's worth spending some time working on desensitising your dog to this particular trigger. Here are some ideas:

- Go to your front door, open door, close it and return
- Go into another room, pause for between 3 and 20 seconds, and return
- Open the front door, go out, come straight back in and return
- Open the front door, go out, pause for varying times, come back in and return

Key point: When doing these exercises, ignore your dog. You're teaching them there is nothing to worry about when these things happen. That these events are no big deal.

STEP 7: Train separations

Training your dog to be happy when you go out and leave them is the the aim of treatment of separation problems.

Like all training, this should be done slowly and gradually, making sure your dog is happy and relaxed throughout. Use a camera or app or record your dog every so often when they're left on their own so you know whether they are showing any signs of stress or not.

Gradually build up the time you leave your dog on their own, very slowly at first by simply going out of a doorway and coming straight back in. Build how long you're out of the room by tiny amounts, a second at a time, always checking your dog is relaxed and happy. Once you have reached a few minutes, you can build the time up by increasing amounts.

This can take a very long time. Be patient and work only at the rate your dog can cope with. Pushing too hard too quickly can make the problem worse.

Once the magic hour mark is reached it should be quicker and easier to increase the time up to 3-4 hours.

It's hard to help your dog learn how to cope with being left alone if they have separation anxiety. It takes a long time to cure the problem and takes dedication from you. So it's inevitable that there will be times you feel like giving up or that you don't feel you're getting anywhere. You'll run through a gamut of emotions too – from delight to despair, frustration to happiness and everything in between.

That's why it's worth getting help from a good dog behaviourist - you'll need support as much as your dog. Our Serene Separation course is available through our online academy (online.downdog. co.uk). The programme takes you through our Seven Steps to Success in detail, covering twelve exercises to help your dog become comfortable when left alone.

If your dog is suffering when left, please help them.

We worked with Lilo over several months. It took time, commitment and significant emotional energy. It was difficult for the owners to manage, finding someone to stay with Lilo when they needed to go out together, but they stuck with the programme and finally, eight months later, they succeeded in being able to leave Lilo for 3-4 hours at a time and she remained calm and happy at home.

Summary

- Separation anxiety is the doggy equivalent of a panic attack
- Train puppies to be happy being left alone from the very start
- Treatment of separation problems works well, but it can take a long time

In the final chapter in this section, we'll look at the common problem of dogs who are afraid of certain noises.

15

NOISE AND OTHER PHOBIAS

Thehe field was right next to people flying model airplanes and just up the hill from Kirkistown racetrack, where there was car racing going on. Gus trotted there quite happily and I was proud of him ignoring the racing, screaming-engined cars. Near the end of our session, rally cars started racing, complete with frequent exhaust gate bangs. Gus's eyes went round and staring, he went tense, and he tried to bolt away. But I couldn't leave - I was in the middle of teaching a nosework class. I struggled to hold him while trying to calm him – my replacement joints aren't really strong enough to resist the massive momentum Gus produces when he lunges in fear. He wouldn't take food and kept twisting and turning, trying to get away – he was too scared to cope. Finally he broke free by backing out of his harness and shot back up the path away from the scary noises. I found him crouched against the car, one of his safe places.

Poor Gus. He's always been highly noise sensitive. Many collies are. I've had to work very hard to help Gus cope with gunshots (there are lots of shoots around us) and other scary noises, like fireworks. He was born on a quiet farm and is a collie, so I wasn't too surprised when he turned out to be noise sensitive from puppyhood (the full story is in my book *Chaos to Calmish*).

I've made huge progress with him but this event was a big setback.

The following day we went to his favourite beach for a walk. Gus was subdued and reacted to every sound he heard by whipping his head round. I had quite a job keeping him engaged with me and coping with the noises, because his stress hormone levels were still quite high after his meltdown the previous day. Do you remember it can take anything up to 48-72 hours for stress and arousal to fully settle?

Dogs can develop a fear of any sound, no matter how inconsequential. A squeaky door being opened, using a fly swatter, dropping a book, clanging a pan lid, or a fan being turned on, can provoke a reaction from a noise-phobic dog. And, the more exposure a dog has to a frightening noise, the more intense his response is likely to become.

Trying to escape from a risky noise, a dog's normal instinctive behaviour is to seek a safe place to avoid danger. That's normal - and sensible. But when the noise is an everyday noise that does not represent a danger, the behaviour can become annoying, frustrating and even dangerous. During thunderstorms, Gus sometimes tries to hide under my desk, in our boiler cupboard, or even, on one memorable occasion, under the TV - and our TV stand has only a 4 inch gap below it.

Gus is also reactive to strong winds, which admittedly can be quite scary around here. Even when you know it's just air moving, the tremendous force of a strong wind can quite literally blow you over. And as for the noise - I have to turn the TV up. Gus is restless while winds are at their height. He isn't quite sure where to settle down - any time he lies down another gust blows and he is up and pacing again. He flatly refuses to go out. Luckily he has incredible bladder capacity and control and can go for 12 hours easily. (I'm so jealous - if I can manage 2 hours, I'm delighted. Age has some drawbacks.)

Gus is also disturbed by heavy rain, car door bangs and similar noises. Other dogs just sleep through these disturbances quite happily.

There are no good figures on just how many dogs suffer from noise sensitivity or phobia, but it is linked to other fears. Of dogs who have separation anxiety, 40% will also have noise phobias.

Your dog will be somewhere on the scale between happily normal, through sound reactive, to sound phobic. Gus is firmly somewhere between the latter two states for several sounds and noises. The difference between fears and phobias is that fear is a normal response to an actual or perceived threat or situation, while a phobia is "an intense and persistent fear which goes beyond a rational response" that occurs when an animal is confronted with something that feels threatening.

Fearful dogs demonstrate the characteristic behaviours of stress. They might seek out a favourite human for reassurance, run away to find a place to hide, or try to escape from the noise by running away, pushing through doors, or even jumping out of windows, or chewing through walls. On one occasion, when frightened by gunshots, Gus tried to dig through a concrete floor.

What sounds does your dog react to?

Sounds vary between high frequency and low frequency types. High frequency sounds include whistles, birds chirping and screaming children. Low frequency sounds include rumbling thunder or bass drums. The volume or amplitude of sound is produced by vibrations. Larger, high energy, vibrations mean louder sounds.

Your dog's hearing is not only more sensitive than yours, but they are also able to hear a wider range of sounds, including both high and low frequency levels.

Common noises your dog may react to include the whistles, whooshes and bangs of fireworks and the staccato explosion of gun shots. The fact that these sounds are intermittent and unexpected contributes to the fear.

Many dogs, like Gus, can be worried or scared by weather noise, especially very heavy rain, hail, strong winds, or the rumbling of thunder. Others may fear the sounds of household machines, or react to other noises, such as musical instruments - a lady once contacted me for help because her dog howled every time her son played his clarinet, a story I'll tell you more about later in the book. Gus reacts in excitement to the muffled thump of the pedal movements when I play the piano, so I have to shut him out of the room at such times.

To help your dog, your first job is to determine what types of sounds your dog is uncomfortable with or reactive to. Watch your dog – they'll tell you. And make a list. Many dogs are worried by more than one sound.

But there are two common myths that I want to bust before I start giving you tips to help your dog.

1) "Don't reassure your dog as it will reinforce the fear". This is a pervasive myth and is nonsense. Always reassure and comfort your dog. You cannot make fear worse through reassurance or cuddles.

2) "Provide a covered crate as it will muffle the sound." It doesn't. Putting a blanket over a crate or even using soundproofing material does not stop sound, especially low frequency sounds like thunder. However, a crate can be useful to provide the feeling of a safe den for your dog.

There are no quick fixes. Slow but sure is the motto for helping dogs with noise fears and phobias. It's practically impossible to completely cure phobias but your aim is to make your dog comfortable and give them options and places where they can feel safe.

How to help your sound fearful dog

If your dog gets worried by the weather, or gets scared by screeches, you can help them by trying these tips:

- make sure they have a safe place to go, preferably one that is covered - a crate with a blanket over it, or a bed behind a sofa, or a covered corner, or under a chair. The covering is to make them feel safer as it doesn't do much at all to muffle sounds.

- move their bed if it's usually by a door or window so they are less bothered by draughts or noise right by their resting place

- play favourite games with them to distract them, and

- give them favourite chews such as a filled Kong or bully stick.

Other things that can help dogs with more severe noise reactions are:

1) Sound masking

Using "white noise" or something similar to help mask the scary noises. The best masks are those with low frequency sounds. You can get apps, or try things like floor fans or tumble dryers with solid (safe) objects such as old trainers in that will rattle round, or even rock music. This only works in the home where you can play such things, of course – and it needs to be something you can cope with, too.

2) Wraps and touch

Some dogs might be helped by using thundershirts (a tight fitting body cover). You can make one out of an old stretchy T-shirt if you have the right size and some sewing skills. The feeling of being swaddled is comforting. Other touch therapies that can help are TTouch or massage. There are courses and books on TTouch which is a programme of particular ways to touch and wrap your dog.

3) Provide a safe place

Find somewhere your dog feels safe. A cupboard, or cellar if you have one, might work. Encourage and help your dog to go there when they're scared. Gus chose our internal, enclosed boiler room during the last thunderstorm.

4) Medication and supplements

If your dog's reaction is very severe and they regularly show significant signs of stress such as panting, wide eyed stare, pacing around and not settling, you might also think about using a calming supplement or medication.

DAP (dog appeasing pheromone) is readily available as Adaptil in diffuser, pump spray, or collar form. Your dog can wear the collar, or a sprayed bandana. Their bedding can also be sprayed. If using a diffuser, plug it in near your dog's "safe" place. It won't help all dogs and in my experience it helps puppies and younger dogs more than older ones, but it is worth a try.

Homeopathic and herbal remedies are a popular and generally safe aid in treating any anxiety-related problem. Natural ingredients such as chamomile, valerian, skullcap and borax may help some dogs to maintain calm and are easily bought in tablet form.

When to give such treatments can be difficult to work out. Most work best if given before the onset of the frightening thing, but giving them at the first sign of a problem may help a bit. And if you have sufficient warning or knowledge that something will happen - for example, firework night, neighbours celebrations, or weather warnings about thunderstorms or severe gales - you can work out when best to give any supplementary help.

Can my dog be cured?

If your dog struggles with loud noises, you're in for the long haul, probably for the rest of your dog's life. Dogs don't 'grow out of' sound sensitivity, and they can develop the problem at any age. Get help from your vet and a good dog behaviourist. Your dog may need drug treatment and you'll probably need to work through a thorough behavioural programme.

The aim is to improve the quality of your dog's life and help them cope better with the scary things.

Drug therapy

Prescribed drug therapy may be required if your dog has moderate to severe fears. This can include several different classes of drugs, including anti-anxiety medications, antidepressants and tranquillisers. Talk to your vet to discuss what might be best for your dog.

Desensitisation

Part of any good treatment programme will include reducing your dog's reaction to scary noises using a desensitisation technique. One option is to use one of the widely available CDs, or you can download tracks of scary noises, such as 'Sounds Scary', available from Dogs Trust in the UK. Or make your own, by recording scary noises where you can, or downloading clips or segments from YouTube videos or similar.

Once you have your recorded sounds ready, here's how to use them:

When your dog is relaxed and enjoying a favourite food or chew toy, start by playing the noise at a very low level where you can barely hear it. Monitor their TEMP (see chapter 7). If your dog shows any negative reaction to the noise, you are playing it too loudly. Turn it down lower.

Repeat playing the noise as frequently as possible; the aim is for your dog to perceive this noise as completely normal and commonplace and to start ignoring it.

Gradually start to increase the volume as your dog's tolerance improves. If at any time they show a negative reaction, go back to the previous level used. Take this training slowly.

Play the noise in as many locations as possible - different rooms in your home, in the car, in friend's houses, or even on walks. Be creative - putting speakers outside your window can go some way towards recreating the effect of real situations.

Understand that this process takes a long time. It may take several weeks or even months of daily practice before your dog is tolerant of the noise.

I've followed this process this with gunshots for Gus. He can now cope pretty well with most gunshots and with far away thunder, but we're still on that long, continual journey to help him. Every incident such as the race track cars sets us back again. I'm cross with myself about that. When I realised what was happening around the field we had to use, I should have just found somewhere quieter to leave Gus. Unfortunately it was a hot day so I couldn't leave him in the car.

These things happen. Expect setbacks. You just have to keep working on it – and I will, because it's horrid feeling panicky and scared, and we all want to help our dogs cope better when they are struggling.

Summary

- Noise sensitivity is common and may be linked to separation anxiety
- Dogs can develop noise sensitivity at any age
- The aim of treatment is to help your dog cope and be comfortable with scary noises

In the next section we'll look at three common problems where otherwise loveable, friendly dogs can irritate and frustrate their owners.

NAUGHTY DOGS

16

WHY DOGS ARE NAUGHTY

I s your dog on the go, all day, every day?

Are they going through a phase of not listening to you, not responding to your cues and generally regressing to puppy behaviours of chewing, biting, barking or whatever?

Perhaps you've got a second (or more) dog but they don't seem to listen to you and are picking up all sorts of unwanted behaviours from your other dog(s)?

Dogs like this are not "bad dogs". They're exasperating, annoying, and frustrating, giving you the run around and making you disheartened and defeated. But they are also loving, fun and entertaining. They are often labelled 'naughty but nice' dogs and this section will help you find some solutions and regain your sanity.

This next short section covers three common problem areas many owners face at one time or another: dogs that are over-energetic and hyperactive, the frustrations of adolescence, and the challenges of having more than one dog at a time. All these issues can drive you to distraction, making you feel frustrated, cross and at the end of your tether.

I'll also give you some tips about your new rescue dog, as rescue dogs are often obtained in adolescence.

17

HYPERACTIVITY

Aspen was a gorgeous, attractive three year old Husky. Her bright eyes were friendly and showed her excitement to meet us and her love for human kind. Emma, her owner, had called us in because Aspen was destroying their home. Emma described how Aspen had been an 'always-on-the-go' dog from being a tiny puppy. She understood the breed and had tried to provide the exercise she knew Aspen needed. She assumed Aspen needed more exercise to tire her out - so by the time we visited, Aspen and Emma were out walking for nearly four hours each day. But Aspen would still not settle at home, pacing round, demanding attention, casually chewing whatever she felt like. Emma was exhausted and had no idea what else to do.

Some dogs are couch potatoes, others are on-the-go all the time. I once knew an Italian Spinone who slept for around 22 hours each day and had to be woken up to go for a walk. Aspen was at the other end of the scale, only settling for a few hours each night.

I have never had anyone complaining about their couch potato dog, but I do get quite a lot of people asking for help because their dog is an over-the-top, crazy idiot. Gus tends towards that end of the spectrum. Like Aspen, from a puppy he never slept much and was active most of the time, although he is sleeping a little more now as he moves into older age.

It's normal for puppies to be on the go. They are excitable and want to explore everything - and this can be exhausting at times. You just want some peace, so you try and force them to rest. But that's a bit like trying to make a 2 year old sit in a chair and colour a book for 2 hours - an impossible dream. Thankfully, this apparently boundless energy generally settles as your puppy works out your household routine.

Excitable dogs will often show their true colours early on. As puppies they continually bite at your hands and fight any attempts to stop them, not just with a minor struggle, but with violent, Houdini-like resistance. Excitable children can encourage and fuel hyperactivity in your dog. Young children tend to run, scream, and wave their arms at nippy, chasing puppies, all of which are guaranteed to escalate your puppy's behaviour. Continued socialisation and novelty are important too; dogs need a certain minimum amount of daily stimulation and activity, such as a good walk, sniff time and training, and can become hyper if this isn't available.

We can flop in front of the TV to relax - it's amazing how hours can pass while we indulge in this mindless activity - but dogs aren't interested in a Netflix binge.

True hyperactivity in dogs is rare. Hyperactivity in dogs is similar to ADHD in people, however, in dogs it's known as hyperkinesis. The hallmarks of hyperkinesis include an inability to relax fully in familiar environments; these dogs will struggle to stay still, can't settle, fidget and move around continually. Dogs with hyperkinesis have exceptionally short attention spans - even shorter than adolescent dogs - and they are highly impulsive. They struggle to focus on any task and are easily distracted. They may be over-reactive to noises, leaping up and barking every time a door shuts, or someone runs past the house. And this reaction occurs every time such an event occurs - these dogs don't seem to get used to things that happen regularly.

Hyperkinetic dogs have high heart rates and may breathe faster than normal. They are especially sensitive to changes in the environment and alterations to their routine. They can overreact to strangers and new animals and may struggle to adjust in new places, or to new situations. They can also be emotionally unstable, becoming aggressive or snapping when stressed and may be almost unmanageable when physically restrained.

You may be reading this and thinking that this describes your dog to a 'T'. In fact, true hyperkinesis is rare. But there are several other causes of, and reasons for, hyperactive behaviour. Read on, as it is one of the following reasons that will probably apply to your dog.

One of the most common causes is learnt behaviour. If your dog has been regularly rewarded for attention seeking behaviour, they are likely to become increasingly demanding. For example, if your dog becomes over-excited when you come home, you may be fuelling that behaviour. Perhaps you always and immediately respond to them and give them a huge fuss. Or you struggle in through the door flapping your arms and telling them to "get down, stop it", or "for goodness sake let me get in first". Soon your dog will be reacting in an over-the-top manner to any family member or visitor, then to other dogs or people passing by. And so the behaviour develops.

Another common cause is territorial behaviour, where your dog tries to protect their boundaries, in the home or in the garden. This can result in excessive reactivity to strange people or animals visiting, or passing by, and your dog barking at anything and everything. Because practice produces progress, allowing your dog to practice this behaviour guarantees it getting stronger and stronger.

Phobias and other anxiety disorders can produce symptoms that are very similar to and can look like over-excitement or hyperactivity.

Never forget that medical conditions may be the cause of any odd or unwanted behaviour in your dog. Always seek your vet's opinion. It's vital to rule out medical causes for excessive behaviour. For example:

- Thyroid disease - 31% of hyperactive dogs were found to have thyroid dysfunction in one study, and
- Chronic lead poisoning - dogs can suffer this from chewing on old linoleum or surfaces painted with lead based paints.

Finally, consider whether the behaviour is due to cognitive decline, a sadly not uncommon problem which tends to surface in older dogs. I'll be covering doggy dementia in detail in book three in this series.

How to help your hyper hound

Treatment for true hyperkinesis is similar to that for ADHD in children. Your vet may undertake a trial of a stimulant. As with children, this will settle a truly hyperkinetic dog, but a dog who is simply overactive will become more so.

Most overactive dogs are simply that, and do not have true hyperkinesis.

Perhaps you've tried to force your pup to have some down time in a crate or quiet room. It doesn't work. Or you've tried to exercise your manic mutt more and more with the aim of tiring them out so they will settle, like Emma. But that doesn't work either - it just makes them fitter so they need even MORE exercise. Aspen was one of the fittest dogs I have ever seen.

High activity levels can be found in any breed, but especially in working, sporting and herding breeds such as Border Collies, Huskies, and working line gundogs - dogs who are physically and mentally active. These dogs can be wearing for their owners if that energy and drive is not properly directed.

So what can you do to help your hyper hound?

1) Check your dogs diet

What your dog eats may have a significant impact on his behaviour - some studies have shown a link between food, sensitivity to some ingredient or other and hyperactivity. There is also some evidence that inadequate nutrition early in life may permanently affect activity levels.

It's tempting to pick up a bag of cheap dog food at the supermarket, but some of the cheaper foods are often loaded with junk stuff such as fillers and colourants. Aim to feed your dog the best quality food you can afford, and add in (safe) occasional fresh fruits, vegetables and left-overs.

When buying dog food, look for a short list of recognisable ingredients, with the protein source being clear and included as meat or meal, a named carbohydrate such as potato or rice, and with minimal fillers and additives. Seek specialist veterinary advice if you are concerned your dog may be reacting to some ingredient in their diet.

Remember, if you decide to change your dogs diet, do so over several days to minimise the chance of gastro-intestinal upset.

2) Review your dogs routine and their environment

A structured day can help your hyper hound by having times for activities and times for calm. Have set times for food games, for training, for mental activities and for rest.

Has your dog got a place of their own where they can go to rest away from the busy traffic of human life? Many people keep their dog's bed or crate in their main living area, but if you have an active family, continually coming in and out, your dog may not be getting the rest they need, which can fuel hyperactive behaviour. Put their bed in a quiet room, or place a covered crate in a quiet corner. Then you will both get some much needed rest.

3) Build in mental exercise

Think about what makes you tired. Going out for a run might (or so I'm told - running is not something that rates high on my agenda.) But if you are an athlete, you may need to run for several miles, or an hour or so, to be tired, which is why Aspen was getting hugely long walks. Trained huskies can run up to 125 miles a day. You can't compete with that.

A brisk walk makes most of us pleasantly relaxed (although this depends on the weather to a large extent) but it is not really tiring. However, working on a report in the office for two hours, or going to a class to learn a new language, or trying to learn a new task, can be exhausting. That's because mental exercise, working our brains, is FAR more tiring per minute than physical exercise. And the same holds true for our dogs.

So if you want to tire your hyper hound, work their brain rather than their body. Here are some ideas:

A) Do some training

Teach your dog a new trick. Train practical skills such as sit, down, and settle. Work on impulse control games such as wait/stay and leave it. Teach your dog to help you with household tasks, such as putting clothes in the washing machine, fetching items for you, tidying their toys away, and so on.

B) Play scent games

Give your dog plenty of opportunities to use their nose. Encourage sniffing on walks. Help them to work through scent based puzzles, and play hide and seek with their toy or favourite treat. Provide at least one meal a day through food toys, scatter feeding, snuffle mats, and food trails. Play search games, or lay short tracks leading to a food or toy play bonus. If you want to learn more about your dog's amazing nose, join a local scent work class. (Look up Scentwork UK, or Talking Dogs Scentwork at scentwork.com.)

c) Do something different

Take up a dog sport such as agility, Rally obedience, hoopers or working trials. You can find out more details about all these online, for example on the Kennel Club website. Search for a club near you that offers training in these sports, which combine physical and mental exercise for your dog - and for you.

At our visit, we spent an hour with Aspen, encouraging her to work out puzzles and use her nose. At the end, she was nearly cross-eyed with fatigue and held up a paw to say she'd had enough. Emma reported that after our visit, Aspen slept for sixteen hours straight. She added mental work into their regular routine. Aspen settled well, sleeping more, and Emma's house has remained pristine since.

Summary

- Over-energetic and excitable dogs are wearing for owners
- All dogs needs quiet rest periods
- A hyper hound needs more brain work, not excessive physical exercise

All dogs can have times when they can be naughty, but the most common problem age, in dogs and in humans, is adolescence, which we'll look at in the next chapter.

18

ADOLESCENCE

S arah was frustrated. Leo was a 7 month old collie terrier cross. He'd been to puppy school and had mastered learning most of the basics, but now Sarah was struggling with some problems. As a puppy, Leo enjoyed plenty of free play with other dogs and Sarah was proud he was so well socialised. But his recall was now non-existent, as he would far rather run off to play with other dogs than come back to her when he was off lead. Squeaky toys and ham weren't doing it for him. He also pulled badly on lead. When he was not getting the attention he wanted he became very barky and would nip Sarah. And despite many tellings off, he simply would not stay off the sofa.

Poor Sarah. Leo had become a teenage tearaway.

Puppies (and children) grow up far too quickly. Adolescent behaviour in dogs starts much earlier than you probably thought, sometimes as early as 18-20 weeks, though more often from around six months of age, and this frustrating stage can last until the dog is around 18 months to two years old.

Adolescence covers the transition from cute bundle of fluff to physical maturity. It is a time of brain maturation – just like in humans. Young dogs like action and speed, they get easily bored when nothing is happening and they have no self-control at all. This means that they often can't control themselves when something exciting happens and they can become over-stimulated and over-excited very easily.

This is a frustrating and difficult time for both humans and dogs. Behaviours seen as cute and funny in tiny puppies become annoying – adolescent dogs become rowdier, mouthier, jumpier and more obnoxious than at any other time in their development. They may develop short fuses and will test you and even ignore you.

During adolescence, hormones start to rage. There is a spike in testosterone especially in male dogs which only starts to reduce to adult levels at around a year to 18 months old. These hormone surges produce bodily changes including rapid growth and body sensitivity. Just as in humans, hormonal changes in dogs can also have a significant effect on behaviour. For example, female dogs can show striking changes in behaviour around their first season, some of it very similar to those seen in pubertal girls.

If you have children you'll be nodding in agreement. From running back home from school, eager to tell you about their day, they become surly and respond only in grunts. They change physically, developing adult characteristics and even have a different smell. From rising with the lark, it becomes a Herculean task to drag them from their beds before midday. And they start to test your boundaries. Big time.

Dogs demonstrate adolescence in very similar ways to children. Instead of responding to your every command and walking nicely on lead, they ignore you, jump up on everyone and everything, pull on the lead and act as if they have never had any training whatsoever. It can feel like walking on eggshells as you try to balance allowing freedom for your dog to blossom, but preventing the rehearsal of unwanted behaviours; encouraging new experiences, but avoiding too much stress.

As your cute puppy morphs into a gangly teenager they develop adult interests. They are more interested in sniffing other dogs, sniffing wee and poo, rolling in smelly stuff, and chasing squirrels, than in responding to you. Your smug pride in your perfect puppy recall can suddenly appear very misplaced. From coming back every time when called, your dog will suddenly start to ignore your calls, screams and pleading, because that rock over there, or the playful pug over here, have become far more interesting than their predictable, familiar owner.

Having started their basic training well, they suddenly won't sit or stay. Some days, they will respond to your cue to 'sit' quite readily. On other days you'll be tearing your hair out because they will look at you as if they have never heard the word before.

This is normal adolescence.

As the owner, you'll need a shed-load of patience during this phase. You'll find you will constantly need to reinforce basic training during adolescence as their previous learning suddenly appears forgotten.

Serious behaviour problems may also emerge during this time. Shy Suzi suddenly starts to lunge and snap at people and growl at visitors; Ludo the Lout gets into scraps with other dogs and is socially obnoxious, posturing, snapping, snarling, growling, and maybe even fighting with other dogs. These problems are often a sign of a lack of confidence and is one of the reasons why continuing socialisation is essential throughout adolescence.

Many dogs can develop new and seemingly irrational fears during this period of their lives, sometimes to things they have been ignoring or happy with previously. Fearful Flora might suddenly see all traffic and, oddly, wheelie bins, as dreadful monsters and refuses to walk where last week she trotted along quite happily.

It is no coincidence that the average age for dogs going into rescues and shelters is around 18 months. A scary statistic is that the majority of dogs euthanised at or before the age of two years old are killed because of behaviour problems, many of which are preventable.

Adolescence is unsurprisingly the most common age for behavioural referrals. Please seek help early if you are worried about your dog's behaviour.

What to do to help your teenage tearaway

Adolescence is about fire fighting. It's a time to go back to basics, repeating and practising all the cues your pup knows, time and time and time again.

Most importantly, decide what you want your dog to do rather than focusing on what they won't do.

The main tool *you* need during your dog's adolescent phase is patience – lots and lots and lots of patience. Then even more. A great sense of humour is also useful.

Here are some tips to help you maintain your sanity during your dogs adolescence:

1) Keep up your socialisation programme

Take your dog to new and different places, to see new and different things and to meet new and different people and other animals. It's important that they see and meet lots of other dogs during this period in their life (while remaining under your control) and that they have positive and successful experiences.

But please be careful about where and with who you allow your dog to play. Unrestricted charging about in a dog park may create and fuel obnoxious, anti-social behaviour as your teenage tearaway with their raging hormones gets into scraps with other dogs. Rather, seek out friends with calm, adult dogs and go for walks and playtimes together. Back up the adult dog if they tell your annoying adolescent off and enforce down time before any behaviour gets out of hand.

2) Gentle, steady exposure to scary things

Your adolescent dog may suddenly become scared of something, or resist going near certain things they previously walked past without a second glance. Make sure they are gently exposed to that/those thing(s) regularly but at a good distance, where you can praise and reward them for being brave and they can learn there is nothing to be scared of. Seek professional help if you are worried, before the problem becomes embedded.

3) Go Back to Basics

Adolescence is a time to go back to basics, repeating and practising all the things your dog knows, time and time again. Focus on achieving rock solid responses to 'come' and 'leave it', because you can control many problem situations with those two cues.

Continue all your basic training, insisting on loose lead walking on walks and good manners in daily life. For example, if your teenage tearaway jumps all over visitors, use a lead to control their exuberance, only allowing greetings when they are calm. Keep sessions simple, short and successful. Adolescence is not the time to teach degree level obedience.

4) Use sensible control methods

It's important to keep your teenage tearaway under control. Using sensible control methods will prevent many problems.

Use a longer lead on walks so your dog can indulge in plenty of sniffing while allowing you to move them rapidly away from rolling in disgusting stuff, pestering people or cavorting with canines.

Keep your dog on a long line when you are on the beach or in the park so that your dog can have some freedom but stay within your control. Call your dog many times during your outings to practice your recall, praising very well every time and making sure you produce rewards that your dog loves. If your dog doesn't respond to your call enforce it if necessary by reeling in your long line.

5) Seek professional help early

If you are at all concerned about your adolescent dog's behaviour please seek help sooner rather than later. Nipping problems in the bud is far easier (and cheaper) than trying to deal with issues once they are established.

Finally, stay positive and upbeat – this time DOES pass. Above all, be considerate and patient - your dog needs time to grow up just as much as adolescent humans do.

A word about rescue dogs

Dogs are most commonly surrendered to rescue as adolescents as noted above. Thus many rescue dogs are obtained by their new families at that difficult 7 to 18 months of age.

Take your time over settling a new adolescent dog into your home and life. It can be challenging for them to adjust into a new home, so be patient. Here is a plan to follow:

1) Give them plenty of time to settle in

Take them on slow, sniffing, local walks for several days, close to your home. Let them learn about their new environment and get used to the smells, sights, noises and activity that will be part of their new lives. Introduce your dog to new places gradually, perhaps one new experience each week or so, rather than bombarding them with novel sights and sounds each day.

Focus on teaching good loose lead walking and responses to basic cues.

2) Set your dog up for success

Decide on your boundaries and rules and stick to them. If you don't want your new dog upstairs, then have your stair gate in place before they arrive. If you don't want your dog on the sofa, block access to your sitting room. Only allow them in the room on lead for the first week or so, so you can teach them your rules from the start.

Agree on what your table rules are going to be. I recommend not feeding dogs from your table at first (or at all if that is your choice), because it's important to teach good food manners. Remember, adolescent dogs push boundaries, so set your rules firmly in place from the start, even if you might want to relax them later on.

3) Avoid overwhelm

Your new dog will become overwhelmed by meeting too many new people at once. Teach good greeting manners from the start, with one person at a time. Allow him to get to know your household first. Then introduce family and close friends gradually. Ask people to visit you, one at a time, over several days.

Slow and sure will yield success.

You'll find help on sixteen common unwanted behaviours you might need to address with your new rescue dog in the first book in this series, Problem Pooch Book 1: Troublesome to Tranquil.

I reassured Sarah that Leo's changed and obnoxious behaviour was normal. We agreed some boundaries for him and Sarah followed the advice given in this chapter.

It wasn't easy - she struggled particularly with controlling Leo's pulling on lead until she introduced 'find it' games on her walks. Setting a strict routine reduced the barky behaviour. The long line worked well, allowing her to regain Leo's previous excellent recall response over a few weeks, and using a lead in the home when visitors came was a game-changer for her. Leo is now the perfect pet they wanted and they are justly proud of him.

Summary

- Adolescence in dogs starts from five or six months of age
- Adolescent dogs will test boundaries and become unresponsive to previously learned cues
- Patience, boundaries and continuing training will help you through this awkward time

Perhaps you've followed all my advice, you haven't had any problems and your current dog is a dream. Therefore, you may be thinking of adding another dog to your family. When you have more than one dog in the same home it can create a range of different problems, which we'll look at in the next chapter.

19

MULTIPLE DOGS

"Just STOP IT," screeched Ellen. Rosie and Rex were having a ball, play fighting and wrestling together, but they had already knocked over a side table and its contents and Ellen was concerned for other fixtures and fittings. "Why did I think getting two puppies was a good idea?" she moaned, "They play well together but they ignore me." Ellen was struggling. Trying to train two puppies at once was exhausting. If she tried taking one out to train, the other screamed the place down, and as for trying to teach them to walk nicely on lead - well, that was like trying to pour tea from a chocolate teapot. She felt superfluous, guilty and frustrated.

When I was a child, centuries ago, people had just one family dog. Those dogs were with people all the time and were friendly, sociable dogs who were often allowed to roam the streets. They were fed on household scraps and got along well together, with just the occasional small and quickly resolved tiff. Many of these dogs were related – if you wanted a pup, there was usually one available somewhere in your neighbourhood from an unplanned mating. There was almost no aggression to humans – if a dog ever growled at or bit someone they were taken behind a shed and shot.

As I've grown up, things have changed. Dogs are no longer allowed to roam free and there are increasingly strict curbs on where dogs can be exercised, with beaches shut off in the summer months and 'on-lead only' rules slapped onto parks and other public spaces.

I've watched with horror the UK bloom of the American practice of dog parks, far-too-small areas where dogs can run free, but often learn and practice all sorts of inappropriate behaviours. Bullies become more proficient, fearful dogs learn aggression to protect themselves, and many dogs become overly dog-focused, leading to recall problems and incurring the wrath of other owners as their precious pooch is pestered by a rambunctious Rover.

But we love our dogs. So much, that multi-dog households are increasingly common. The average number of dogs in dog-owning households is now 1.4 in the UK and 1.3 in Northern Ireland (2019 data) and in the USA it's 1.6 (2020 data).

Having more than one dog in the home brings its own set of problems and issues, as Ellen was finding. More than one dog equals having a pack (I'm using the word here to mean a group) and, just like having children, two need at least twice the time, effort, energy and cost of one.

Many people have multiple dogs and manage well, with humans and dogs co-existing peacefully and happily. But it takes commitment and work.

As my friend Sarah Bartlett, author of *Another Pup? A comprehensive guide to adding to or becoming a multi-dog household* says, "I don't know of any perfectly-behaved multi-dog households and I'm not sure they exist. Having multiple dogs and preventing them from becoming a pack of wild dogs who you happen to live with and provide food for, is very hard work. The more you have, the harder work it is to get it right and keep it that way."

My advice is to think long and hard before getting a second (or more) dog.

If you want another dog, there are several things to consider in order to get it right.

All animals have five key welfare needs:

- The need for a suitable environment
- The need for suitable diet
- The need to exhibit normal behavioural patterns
- The need to be housed with, or apart from, other animals, and
- The need to be protected from pain, suffering and disease.

Note the fourth need. This need, about being housed with other animals, is perhaps what people who want more than one dog are thinking about. But that need is really about companionship and to ensure dogs are not kept in isolation away from other beings, not about dogs living with other dogs.

Contrary to the still popular belief, dogs are not pack animals. (Neither are wolves, by the way, who form family groups, not packs.) Studies of village feral dogs show that they live as individuals, coming together with others only for a specific purpose, such as hunting large prey, or copulation (sex). Most feral individuals are solitary scavengers that participate with others for only brief periods, under a rigid hierarchy. When feral dogs do group together, the 'pack' has up to ten members, consisting of two males and six to eight females. A feral dog pack typically lasts only between one and two and a half weeks.

Dogs do not need, or often want, to live with other dogs.

Why do you want another dog?

There are three common reasons for wanting another dog.

One common reason is 'because I think my first dog will be happier with another dog to play with and keep them company.' And this is also the worst reason. Your dog does not need another dog to play with or to keep it company. That's your job. Providing entertainment and company is what owners are for and what dogs have been bred for – to be a human's best friend. Which is why I don't like to see pet dogs kept outside in a kennel. Dogs need regular and prolonged interactions with their human family.

If you don't have time for your current dog, you'll never find time for more.

Another reason for getting a second dog is if your first dog is not happy being left alone and suffers from separation distress or anxiety. You might feel your dog will be happier with another dog while you're out. Sadly, adding another dog rarely makes a difference and your initial dog will continue to pine for your company. It's best to sort that problem out first before considering getting another dog.

The final reason you may want another dog is because your current dog is getting older and you don't want to be dog-less. This is a valid reason. Or perhaps you always wanted more than one dog, like me.

When I got my first dog, Ben, we had planned always to have two dogs. We knew enough not to get two together at least. We got Bill, our second dog, when Ben was around fifteen months old. There is great joy in watching your dogs play together - we were lucky and they got on well. Whenever Ben had had enough of Bill pestering him, Ben would simply sit on top of him. They were completely different characters. I did a lot of training with both of them - I competed with Ben in working trials and with Bill in obedience. This was before I had children, so I had the time to do it and, more by luck than judgement, it worked.

Potential problems with more than one dog

If you moved on your own to France but didn't speak French, you'd really try hard to learn enough of the language to be comfortable living there and be able to communicate and have someone to talk to. But if you moved there with your family, you'd have people to talk to and you'd probably not bother so much about learning the language.

That's exactly what can happen with a second dog. A second dog will naturally look to the first dog for help and guidance as to how they should live in this new life. All too frequently, they never learn our human language, and sadly may not bond well with their owner. Rather, the second dog just copies whatever the first dog does.

Getting two dogs together compounds that problem. And it's simply impossible to train two puppies at the same time, as Ellen quickly found out.

But possibly a worse difficulty is that there's no guarantee that your current dog will want to live with your new dog, or vice versa.

Perhaps your current dog is a friendly dog who enjoys meeting other dogs when out on walks and is sociable and comfortable with the other dogs they meet. Equally, I'm sure you are able to tolerate and be polite to the majority of people you meet – but you wouldn't want to live with most of them.

Dogs are the same. They may be happy meeting and playing with other dogs out and about, but it's a very different thing to have to live permanently with another dog in your house. Your dog will usually tolerate another dog being brought into the family, but not necessarily enjoy it.

You might think the new dog will learn good manners from the existing dog. More often, the opposite happens. Niggles that you've lived with become bigger problems as each dog encourages the other to practice all sorts of normal dog behaviours you usually don't want.

For example, whenever a client needs help with a dog who's reactive to other dogs, our first question is "How old is your other dog?" Nearly all the reactive dogs I see, 99%, live with another, older dog and have become reactive because they have never developed sufficient social skills of their own, or built enough self-confidence.

Living with another dog is not socialisation. Instead, nervousness or fear of other dogs may go unnoticed because your new puppy 'hides' behind the other dog (in an emotional sense), relying on their company when other dogs or people approach. Reactivity then appears during adolescence as the dog moves into social maturity.

Having more than one dog at a time is hard work, so if you are truly committed to the idea, set yourself up for success by following the tips below.

How to add another dog successfully

Here are some tips to help you get it as right as you can:

1) The Rule of Four

Using the "rule of four" formula gives you the best chance of ending up with a harmonious household. In other words, the more differences between your dogs the better, because that will help minimise the potential for problems. In her book, Sarah recommends a minimum four year age gap and getting a different breed or breed type. In general, getting a dog of the opposite sex is best and, ideally, a dog with a different character to your current dog. Sarah's book, *Another Pup? A comprehensive guide to adding to or becoming a multi-dog household* contains a detailed description of the common dog functional characters.

2) One at a time

Please, never, ever, introduce more than one dog at a time and certainly not two puppies at once. As Ellen found, it is more than a full time job trying to raise two puppies together. Everyone I've ever known who has tried this has sworn never, ever to do it again.

Going from one dog to two is hard enough but going from two to three is the biggest jump – it changes everything. Do thorough research, be prepared, and ask for help early if you need.

3) Prevent your new pup pestering your older dog

It is not your current dog's job to discipline your new puppy and teach it manners - it's yours. Your current dog may put up with and tolerate the new puppy for your sake, but it is not fair to allow them to be disturbed and pestered. Protect your older dog. Make sure your new pup has plenty of play time with you and that you take time to teach them your house rules and how you want them to behave.

4) Make the additional dog an only dog at first

Treat your new pup as if they are your only dog for several months, ideally the whole first year. This is the best way to ensure your new pup grows into the perfect pet you want. Play with and walk each dog separately. Allow your dogs to interact only for short periods. Baby gates are useful as they can keep the dogs separate but allow them to smell, hear, see and get used to each other without fear of a scuffle and means your older dog can rest and snooze without needing to worry about the new pup.

5) Keep to a routine

Make sure your existing dog's routine remains stable. Spend time with them on their own, keep to their usual walks and playtimes. Make the transition as easy as possible for them - after all, they didn't ask for the new interloper to arrive. It will put their noses out of joint and they'll need your reassurance and the comfort of a known routine.

At risk of sounding like a broken record, please seek professional help early if you hit any problems. Most problems can be sorted out given time, patience and effort.

But - thankfully rarely - some dogs just don't get on despite you trying everything.

Sadly, if it goes wrong and the dogs just can't get on together, you will have to make some difficult choices. You have only three viable options, none of which are ideal and all of which are likely to cause you (and the dog) angst and heartache:

- Keep both dogs but keep them separated for the rest of their lives. This requires an incredible and almost impossible level of management, care and time as you'll need to do everything twice over
- Re-home one dog – to rescue, a friend or a family member who are willing to take them
- Euthanasia - putting a dog to sleep. An horrific and difficult decision to have to make at any time.

~

Ellen sought our help. She struggled with finding the time, patience and energy to deal with the two pups separately, but to her great credit, she worked hard and did her best. They are now lovely adult dogs who she adores, but she is the first to plead with others never to do what she did.

Summary

- Think as carefully before getting another dog as you did before getting your first one - or even more so.
- Be prepared for the significant time and effort that will be involved for a considerable period.
- Plan ahead for potential problems and seek help early

One of the problems Ellen faced was barking whenever Rex and Rosie were playing together. In the next section we'll look at all the different noises dogs make, why they occur and what to do.

VOCALISATIONS

20

WHY NOISY BEHAVIOURS ARE SO ANNOYING

Dogs can produce an amazing variety of sounds and noises – and some dogs produce way more than others!

Barking, and all the grunting, whining, squealing and other noises your dog can make, are normal. They are important ways in which dogs communicate. We humans use our voices to show emotion such as excitement, displeasure, anger, fear, and friendly greetings. Dogs use their voices for very similar reasons.

Some people are quiet, saying very little. Some people are loud and verbose, seemingly in love with their own voices, always quick to break a silence and happy to talk to everyone and anyone - all the time. Other people are silent and mysterious. I'll let you decide where on that spectrum I sit…

Dogs are the same. Some dogs are far more vocal than others. One of my previous dogs, Bryn, only barked about three times in his whole life, whereas Gus barks at least three times every day - and sometimes every hour.

If you ask your friends what noises dogs make, most people will say barking. Some might add whining or howling, but in fact there are many different noises dogs can make.

Here's a brief summary:

Whining or whimpering

These sounds often communicate that the dog is not in emotional balance in some way. They might be fearful or under stress, excited, or expectant.

Howling

Howling is a dog's equivalent of making a long-distance phone call. It can be plaintive, similar to how we sometimes describe plaintive cries in ourselves - you might describe a child as howling when they are very upset. Or it may be more of a "Hello? Anyone there?" type of howl, which is more curious or questioning than upset sounding.

Screaming

Nova Scotia Duck Tolling retrievers, often called Tollers, have a very specific type of vocalisation. Their name comes from their ability to Toll - luring or enticing ducks from their hiding places. Tollers have a penetrating scream that they produce to indicate excitement and eagerness. To the uninitiated, this can sound like the dog is being fed into a shredder; it is high pitched, frantic, and loud.

A scream that sounds like a child in pain can also be a sign of pain and panic from a dog who is fearful for its life. This noise is usually triggered by an acute, dramatic event. One client I had was letting her dog run round the garden while we chatted. The next moment the dog was screaming - in doing the zoomies round a flower bed, the dog had subluxed a patella (knee cap) and we had to rush her to the vets for treatment.

Yipping

Quick rapid short, sharp yips may be a breed characteristic – often heard from small companion breeds. Small dogs may yip for attention, yip in excitement, yip in distress, or yip as a warning. Context is everything.

Distress yipping sounds like 'yip-yip-yip-howl', where the howl element is more prolonged. This is often triggered by isolation from dog or human company and again is most often found in small breeds who hate being left alone.

Yelping

A single yelp, similar to a short, high-pitched bark, is a response to a sudden unexpected pain, shock or surprise. You might hear it if you tread on your dog's paw by mistake, or they catch a paw in a door, or tear a nail. Gareth's dog Tippi yelped last week when chasing a ball and he found she had torn her dew claw. She was very sorry for herself. I once caused a dog to yelp in surprise when I grabbed their harness to stop them running off. Odd yelps like this can be common.

A series of yelps indicates an ongoing response to fear or pain.

Sighing

A sigh is a simple emotional signal that terminates an action – it's very similar to what humans do, too. If the action has been rewarding, it signifies contentment. Or a sigh of relief can signal the end of an effort or completion of some demanding task.

Growling and snarling

Growling and snarling are warning noises. Dogs will use these sounds when they feel threatened, when they want to threaten a potential intruder, or when they want a person or another dog to keep their distance. They signify that the dog is prepared to escalate their behaviour if the person or animal the dog is directing the behaviour towards doesn't take some action to de-escalate the situation.

In general, low-pitched sounds (such as a dog's growl) indicate threat, anger and the potential for aggression. These often mean 'Stay away from me.' High pitch sounds can mean the opposite, either the dog asking to be allowed to come closer or saying that they are happy for you to approach.

Growling can also occur when dogs are playing, with you or with another dog, often during a tug game. A play growl is a very different sound to a warning growl. It's higher pitched, varies in tone and has no aggressive intent at all.

Barking

All dogs bark. It's part of normal canine communication. Barking is the equivalent of human conversation, used to attract the attention of another dog or human. It announces a dog's intention and very often helps relieve stress. Dogs don't just bark when they are warning about something, or they are excited. They can also bark when they're annoyed, surprised, irritated, frightened, or plain lonely.

Barking is a huge topic because of the myriad of reasons why dogs bark, which is why the rest of this section of the book is mainly devoted to different barking problems.

Barking isn't a problem for the dog, but it can be a problem for you, especially if you live close by neighbours who get irked by it.

It's a common unwanted behaviour. It's downright annoying. It's disruptive, can make you jump if you're not expecting it, will interrupt you when you are working, and can upset other people. Excessive barking can be a problem in certain breeds. And barking amongst dogs in kennels is commonplace.

Barking as a problem behaviour is most commonly barking that occurs in the home. The trigger for people seeking help can be owner frustration, but is often a neighbour complaint, either to the owner directly or to the council as a noise nuisance.

We had one case where the owners contacted us, very concerned because their neighbours had complained to the local council about their dog barking when it was left alone at home. When we went along to assess this dog we were surprised with what we found. The dog was perfectly normal; quiet and relaxed when left alone and I could find no behaviour problem at all. We set up video and audio recordings which showed that the dog barked three times, each a single bark at an outside noise, during the whole time he was left, a four hour period. The rest of the time he lay down and snoozed. My advice to the owner was to ignore the neighbour as there was no way any sensible council officer could uphold the complaint once we gave them our findings.

Does your dog bark? What do you do?

Barking is reinforced by the consequence - what happens as a result of the barking. Most barking is reinforced either by the owner's reaction to it (shouting "Shut UP!", or "Be Quiet!"), or by what happens in response to the barking – it makes the postman go away, or keeps another dog from getting too close, for example.

A common reason for people to ask for help is their dog being too noisy. The questions is always "How do I stop my dog barking (or howling, or whatever)?" A more appropriate question to ask is "Why is my dog barking?"

Summary

- Dogs can produce a wide variety of sounds

- Some dogs are far more vocal than others
- Barking is a common unwanted behaviour

In the remaining chapters of the book we'll look at different types of problem noises dogs can make, the common reasons for barking and discuss what to do about them. We'll start by looking at that mournful, piercing noise, howling.

21

HOWLING

C*lare was puzzled. Her dog, Merry, was a wonderful pet the majority of the time, obedient, playful and very much part of the family. But he had one very odd habit. Clare's son played the clarinet and every time he practised it, Merry would sit and howl mournfully. Her son was annoyed because he felt Merry didn't like his playing, but Clare thought there was something more going on. She wrote and asked me why Merry did it and what she could do about it.*

Howling is a normal dog sound, though used far less often than barking. Some dogs never howl. Canids in the wild - wolves, dogs, coyotes and others - use howling to communicate with others, either when separated from them, or when gathering the group together for travel or hunting.

Young puppies will often howl when first introduced to a crate at night. Their lives have been turned upside down, they've been taken away from everything they've ever known and they are all alone, with no mum or siblings to comfort them. It's no wonder many pups are very scared and frightened and they may well howl, possibly trying to contact their doggy family. (Check out my books, *Pesky Puppy to Perfect Pet* and *Please May I Have a Puppy* for the best ways to help a new puppy settle quickly.)

Some dogs hate being shut away and will howl from frustration or boredom. Being shut in a room, kennel or crate, enforces separation from the family, so quite often howling can be a sign of separation distress. This does need attention and action, because if nothing is done it may get worse and the dog might end up hurting itself trying to escape from the enforced confinement.

If your dog struggles with being left alone, re-read chapter 14 and please ask for professional help.

But back to howling.

Why dogs howl

Howling is a dog's equivalent of using the telephone – it's how your dog communicates with dogs in other places, even when they are a great distance away. It acts as a type of homing beacon, by identifying a particular location. The noise can also be a warning, communicating that the particular place or territory has been claimed and is occupied, and intruders should keep away.

Hunting dog breeds such as Beagles and various hounds howl when in pursuit of prey or to call the pack together when the prey has been cornered.

There are two main, different types of howling. A sing-song howl is used to contact other dogs and means that the dog is curious or happy. A plaintive, mournful howl may signal that the dog is bored or in distress; dogs sometimes howl when they're hurt or ill.

Some dogs howl when they are happy, especially the northern breeds such as Malamutes and Huskies - they might howl when you arrive back home after an absence because they are so happy to see you return. Some dogs howl in response to high pitched sounds, certain frequencies, or particular combinations of sounds and frequencies, such as emergency vehicle sirens.

Howling at certain regular noises like a television programme theme tune, a particular radio jingle, or music practice, is often amusing to owners. But it can be a problem if it is interrupting and distracting - and it can be hard enough getting children to practice their instruments anyway.

One of my previous dogs would howl if we howled at him in a high pitched voice. One of my friends had a dog that howled at the EastEnders theme tune. Every time.

Gus has an odd habit of howling in the morning when I turn the shower on. It is very specific to that trigger. It started when he was a tiny puppy and has continued. I suspect it is something to do with the specific sound or tonal mix of the shower motor – perhaps it sounds like another dog howling and Gus feels he has to join in. I don't know for sure. Howling often sounds sad, but Gus is quite content when he howls at the shower.

I wonder if some types of howling might be related to anticipation - for example, Gus's shower howling could be because he knows that we're getting up and will soon be coming downstairs.

So what can you do?

If your dog suddenly starts howling, or howls more than usual, take them to a vet for a check up to rule out illness or injury before doing anything else.

Howling from loneliness or boredom can be helped by you spending more time with your dog, making sure they have satisfying sniff walks and plenty of mental work such as training or scent work. Mental work can be as simple as searching and foraging for their food - using snuffle mats, food trails or other food games. Getting help from a dog walker or dog sitter might also be an option if you have to leave your dog for long periods and you suspect their howling is due to to boredom and/or loneliness.

If your dog howls in response to certain noises such as sirens or particular tunes, they will usually stop when the noise stops. This type of howling is not generally a huge problem. But if it is disruptive, such as Merry's howling at clarinet practice times, you can try giving your dog a food toy such as a filled Kong in another room whilst the noise continues. Or you could teach your dog to fetch a toy and play with you instead of howling.

Howling for attention can be more difficult to manage. It's important not to respond to your dog at all while they are howling for this reason as it will reward the behaviour and strengthen it. Ignore the howling but make sure you *do* pay your dog attention when they are *not* howling - which is easier said than done. Please note that at first the howling might get worse - because after all, this behaviour has worked up to now. Grit your teeth and persevere.

Dogs that howl because they feel stressed by, or are reactive to, a particular sound or frequency often gets worse over time and will need help. The aim of treating these dogs is to change the emotion they feel by a dual process we dog trainers love, called desensitisation and counter conditioning, described earlier in this book - basically it means changing how your dog feels about the trigger and changing how they respond to it. Please ask for professional help if this is the problem you are struggling with.

Sometimes you need really good detective skills to work out what might have started your dog howling and what is making it continue. Ask for help from a behaviourist if you need.

I explained to Clare the reasons why Merry might be howling. Giving Merry a lickimat and chew toys in the utility room during clarinet practice reduced the howling. And Clare's son accepted that Merry was never going to be the greatest fan of his music.

Summary

- Howling is often used to attract attention or signify an emotional state
- Certain common sounds can trigger howling
- It is usually self-limiting, but do seek advice if it is a problem

Slightly less disruptive than howling, but equally annoying, are dogs who whine or cry. We'll look at these problems in the next chapter.

22

WHINING AND CRYING

T he garden gate opened. Gus shot to the window and produced an odd noise, a sort of moan-whine-yodel "Yowel-wowel-owel-wowel". Gareth and Tippi had arrived and walked across the courtyard. Gus was poised at the door to greet them, giving a breathy "Hooooooo-ah-hooooo", a type of whine-howl-yawn, to signal his pleasure and excitement at something that interrupted his humdrum routine.

Whining or whimpering usually communicate that the dog is not in emotional balance in some way and that they are worried or concerned by something. The louder or more prolonged it is the greater the emotion behind it.

In pet dogs, whining is often triggered by excitement or expectation, such as in Gus's case above, of something the dog knows is about to happen. Gus sometimes whines in anticipation when we are about to put his harness on, as he knows this signals a walk and often a favourite ride in the car. But other emotions such as stress, fear, anxiety, or boredom can also be a cause of whining.

Whining is especially common in puppies, as they learn how to communicate their needs and wants. Young puppies whine in soft whimpers to get attention and food from their mother in the same way that babies cry.

Older dogs can continue that habit as a way to get human attention. Whining for attention can be communicative - and plain annoying. Perhaps your dog whines to get food, whines for you to throw the ball, whines for you to give them a fuss, whines to be let out of their crate, whines when they want water, whines to go out, whines to come in, and generally whines for whatever it is that they want at the time. Perhaps they want a piece of whatever you are eating - this type of whining has usually been caused (and rewarded) by you giving in to those pleading, mournful, big brown eyes previously. One of my previous dogs, Ben, whined determinedly whilst staring into my face when he had lost his toy under the settee and wanted me to get it out for him.

Dogs who whine as you prepare to leave them and/or when

they are alone, may have separation distress or anxiety. In these cases you may also see them display other symptoms, such as pacing and panting, or more severe symptoms such as drooling, elimination, or destruction as we discussed in a previous chapter.

Dogs may whine in response to discomfort or illness, or when they are wounded and in pain. I had a previous dog who started whining and looking uncomfortable after eating. It turned out that he had a food allergy and a change of food cured the whining. Whining from pain or illness is usually obvious when the cause is acute, but if you notice that your dog starts to vocalise regularly, or they start producing different sorts of whines than usual, it's important to take them to the vet to rule out a medical cause.

Some dogs whine at night. This could mean they are in pain from arthritis or another musculoskeletal problem, or have some other health issue, which is why night whining is often worse in older dogs. Or it may be that your dog needs more help and training to be relaxed at night on their own.

As always, context is everything.

What does your dog's whine mean?

Working out the reason for your dog's whining or crying can sometimes be difficult. Here are some tips:

- Whines that result from loneliness are soft and mournful and pull at your heart strings.
- Attention whines sound a bit like noisy yawning and may be accompanied by a widely opened mouth.
- If your dog is in pain, stressed, fearful or worried, they may produce repetitive whines with occassional shrill yaps.
- Whining that rises in pitch and ends in a sort of yelp is usually a request or plea for something.

- Whining that drops in pitch or fades away usually indicates excitement and anticipation, such as when greeting a friend, waiting for food to be served, or expecting a ball to be thrown.
- Whining that occurs during greetings (of people or dogs) is usually caused by excitement.

Other greeting whines include what can be interpreted as appeasement behaviour - a behaviour aimed at reducing a potential threat from another being. When interacting with people or other dogs, these dogs whine as they lower their body and head, tuck their tail in and avert their gaze. The dog is saying that they are no threat and just want to say hello.

While whining can be annoying, like all the other noises your dog makes, it is communication. Your dog is trying to tell you something—you just need to work out what it is.

What you can do about whining

What you do about whining depends on the reason your dog is whining. Here are some tips for dealing with different whines.

1) Attention whines

Whining for attention can be persistent - and highly annoying. If you respond to that pleading noise each time you will reinforce that behaviour and it will become more frequent. And louder. Because it works.

To reduce the behaviour you need to gird your loins, stand strong and ignore it. Don't give in to the whining and don't reward the behaviour, which includes not looking at your dog, not touching them and not talking to them. Concentrate on waiting until they are quiet, then shower them with attention, fuss and praise.

For example, if your dog whines to be let out of their crate, don't move towards the crate or even look, until they are quiet. As soon as there is quiet, reach towards the crate door. If your dog starts up again, remove your hand and step back. Wait for quiet. Only when they are quiet should you open the crate door to let them out. This will take a long time the first time, especially if the whining has achieved results for your dog in the past. But if you stick it out, it will gradually take less and less time for your dog to be quiet, and the whining will stop.

Follow the same procedure for dogs who whine for you to throw a ball. Or if your dog whines to be let outside, teach them an alternative behaviour, such as to ring a bell, instead. And make sure your dog's water bowl is always full - an empty bowl is a trigger for Gus to whine. Followed by kicking it round the room if the whine doesn't work.

2) Worried Whines

These whines can occur when your dog is frightened, anxious or stressed. They will usually show other signs of fear, or may try to avoid or get away from whatever is causing them to be afraid. Try to work out what is causing the stress or fear using the information in the first part of this book to help you.

To address this type of whining, follow the advice given in earlier chapters. Work slowly, and don't rush the training. It takes time to teach your dog that scary things are not so scary after all. If you need help, contact a professional, reward-based behaviourist.

The key to helping a dog who whines from stress or worry is to address the source of the fears and anxieties.

3) Excitement Whines

These are dogs who whine when you grab their lead, when they're in the car, when you pick up a favourite toy, when you're approaching a favourite place—basically any time they get excited, particularly if there's a wait for them to get what they're expecting. And remember, the more your dog practices their whining the better they get at it - and the behaviour becomes ingrained.

These dogs whine because these items, situations or places have immediate meaning. The appearance of the lead, or a toy, or being in the car, or arriving at a favourite place predict something the dog loves is about to happen, hence the excitement whining.

You may not be bothered by these noises, but if you are, the key to stopping this behaviour is to break the link between the events. For example, if your dog whines when you pick up their lead, you could leave it lying around somewhere you walk through regularly, such as a hallway or kitchen. Every time you pass the lead, pick it up, jiggle it around and put it down again. You can even attach the lead to your dog, count to three and take it off again. With enough repetition, the lead will stop being the predictor of the exciting walk or car ride and your dog will stop whining when the lead appears. You can use a similar method with toy and with car excitement whining.

For example, you can take your dog to the car, let him in, sit in it yourself then both get out again. If it is the car moving that causes the whining, you can try various methods - stop the car as soon as the dog whines (if it is safe to do so, obviously) and only drive on when your dog is quiet. Or travel with a passenger who can reward your dog for being quiet and not whining. Or try giving your dog a food toy such as a stuffed Kong. You can practice with very short trips - drive down your driveway and back up again, or drive down the road and come straight back, or drive round the block then come home - you get the idea.

For excitement whining on arriving at a favourite place, you can drive to the place, stop in the car park and read a chapter of a book or listen to a short podcast before getting out for your walk. Or don't go for a walk at all - come straight back home.

You may not feel you want to bother addressing this behaviour - and that's fine, too.

4) Alert whining

Some dogs will whine instead of bark when they hear a noise or when someone passes the door, or they hear a cat or other animal intruder in the garden. The approach to this is the same as for dogs who alert bark, which we'll cover later on. In summary, the procedure is to thank your dog for alerting you to the intruder or visitor, wait for quiet, then give a reward.

For dogs who whine because they are watching the exciting

events happening in the world through a wide-screen-TV-window or glass front door panels, then preventing access to their entertainment will reduce the whining.

5) Whining due to pain or injury

This type of whining should never be ignored. If your dog is acting strangely, their breathing has changed, or they are not eating or eliminating, seek veterinary help immediately.

Sometimes the whining starts or builds gradually over several days or weeks. This type of whining may indicate a more chronic illness of problem, such as pain from arthritis or pain from some internal cause. Arrange a vet appointment for a full check over.

6) Whining during greetings

If your dog whines briefly when greeting their favourite people, like Gus does, you may not want, or need, to take any action. But if the behaviour annoys you, or is excessive, then there are several things you can do.

The first is to tone down greetings. Rather than your visitor immediately bend down to fuss the dog or ruffle their fur, ask the visitor to take their coat off, or put down their bag, and walk further into the house. Ask them to wait until the dog is calm and quiet before greeting them gently. Downplay those greetings and keep them short and simple.

You can also teach your dog to do something you'd like them to do instead of whining, such as sitting when they greet you or other people, or fetching a toy. Giving your dog a polite behaviour to focus on will often reduce or stop the whining.

7) Whining when left alone

Dogs who whine when they are left alone have some level of separation distress or anxiety. Please follow the advice given in the earlier chapter and seek professional help early if it is a problem or your dog is suffering.

Summary

- Whining is often triggered by excitement or expectation, but it can also indicate the dog is in distress
- Different types of whines have different meanings
- Use the tips given to help with whining in different circumstances

In the next chapter we'll start looking at the most common form of annoying noise your dog can make - barking.

23

BARKING

V*egetating in front of the TV, I was sprawled on the sofa when suddenly there was a loud crash outside. Gus leapt up and barked madly "woo-woo-woo-woo-woo-woo". Then he paused, cocked his head to one side, paced around between the window and door, then finally wandered back to the sofa and settled again. My heart rate took considerably longer to settle and the coffee I'd spilt took a while to mop up. Investigating outside, the noise was from a large plant pot falling over in the strong wind. I moved it round the corner where it was more sheltered and made a mental note to ask Himself to site it somewhere better in future, or weigh it down more.*

Barking is a natural dog behaviour and is a fascinating subject. People originally thought barking was simply a loud, obnoxious thing dogs did, but we know now this is not the case. Research has shown there are specific bark subtypes and that barks have the potential to communicate detailed information to both dogs and people.

Lassie, the famous TV dog, apparently communicated specific information like, "Timmy's stuck in the well! The one in the corner of the yard. You gotta save him!" Sorry to burst a childhood fantasy, but dogs can't do this.

Barking is a normal and natural means of canine communication (along with whining, howling and growling). All domestic dogs have the ability to communicate by barking. Their barks can mean, "I'm shut out and I want in," or "My toy's stuck under the sofa," or "Intruder alert! Intruder alert!"

Just like some people are quiet and some have verbal diarrhoea, some dogs hardly bark at all and some are barking mad. Any dog breed, and any dog, can bark excessively. But all dogs can be trained to be calm and quiet.

Some breeds can be highly vocal, commonly Beagles, German Shepherds, Yorkshire terriers, Miniature Schnauzers, West Highland White terriers and Dachshunds. You may noticed there is a preponderance of terrier breeds in that list. A terrier's job is to hunt, usually underground, so barking is important to tell their owner where they are if they get stuck.

Although it helps to know the individual that you are communicating with, it's not essential, particularly when it comes to hunting. Packs of dogs, such as Beagles and foxhounds, that have been selectively bred to hunt as a team, rely on vocal communication when they find quarry by using a particular type of bark, baying, to alert the other pack members.

Hunting is not the only time that dogs use vocal communication with each other and bark as a group. Anyone who runs a dog training class will be able to tell you that it only takes one 'alarm bark' in the group and every dog in the room will join in.

Barking is strongly linked to nurture. For example, puppies born to a mother who practises alarm barking – a dog who gives a series of rapid, high-pitched barks when someone comes to the door, or passes the house – will almost certainly copy that behaviour later in their own lives.

Some dogs bark as an attention-seeking behaviour, or as a result of excitement. Barking may be a symptom of a reactive nature (such as dogs who bark at every little noise), it may be a learned response, and it can develop as a habit. For example, Gus barks when I sit on my study chair – I've explained in my book, *Chaos to Calmish*, how that began and how I neglected to deal with it at the time it started, so it is now an ingrained and annoying habit that I have to manage.

Barking can relate to all sorts of environmental situations and influences. We'll look at some of these in detail in this section of the book. Noisy behaviour may also have a physiological basis, such as barking that is related to canine cognitive dysfunction (doggy dementia). More about that in book 3 in this series.

But a bark is not just a bark. There are many different types of bark. I'm sure you've noticed some in your own dog, There are single barks, multiple barks, deep threatening barks, higher-pitched playful barks, and many more.

Types of bark

It's difficult to describe sounds in text, but I'll have a go as this might give you some help in identifying the type of bark your dog is producing.

An alert bark is the most common form of barking. It consists of rapid strings of a few barks with pauses between, something like "woof-woof-woof, woof-woof-woof-woof, woof-woof-woof". It sounds urgent and means something like: 'Something's going on that should be looked into.'

The "woo-woo-woo-woo-woo" bark in response to a loud noise is a startle/warning bark - rapid, frequent barks in a short sequence, which may be repeated more than once. Its aim is to warn others in the vicinity that there might be a danger nearby, so be alert. Warning barks can happen when your dog hears an unusual noise, or is uncertain of the origin or cause of the sound it has heard. This was the type of bark Gus did at the plant pot falling over. The dog will give this "woo-woo-woo-woo-woo-woo" bark, then pause to listen if any other dog in the neighbourhood has also noticed anything. You may notice a chain reaction of nearby dogs responding and barking in the same way, which may well set your pooch off again.

But this is not the same as an alarm bark.

If I woke up in the middle of the night because I thought I'd heard a noise downstairs, I would not leap from my bed and shout and yell. No, I'd poke Himself awake and whisper, "I'm sure I heard a noise downstairs. You need to go and see what's going on." In other words, I want to alert the household to a potential danger, but I don't want to let the intruder know where I am and risk being murdered in my bed.

A canine alarm bark does pretty much the same thing. It's usually a single, low, sound – often so quiet that you miss it ("grr-woof"). It may or may not be followed by the dog then giving a volley of defensive or alert barks. If other dogs hear that sound, then in response they will take up arms with a cacophony that's truly impressive – although none of them probably know what they're actually barking about.

Barking in a fairly continuous string but at a lower pitch and slower than the usual alert bark, with some longer pauses, suggests that your dog is sensing some imminent problem. It means something like "I'm not quite sure what's happening, but be ready for action."

A series of high pitched barks may mean your dog is worried and wants attention - it means "Help please! I'm in a spot of bother here."

A low, slower, repetitive bark – the sort your dog will often make when a stranger approaches – means that your dog is feeling defensive, concerned or threatened. This sort of bark is often accompanied by the odd growl or growl-like noise.

One or two sharp short barks at a high or midrange pitch is a typical greeting bark. This bark usually replaces the alarm bark when your visitor is recognised as friendly. Many people are greeted in this way by their own dog when they walk in the door after a short absence.

Quick, repetitive, high-pitched barks can mean that your dog has spotted something that has excited them, or that they want to play a game, or chase something, or that they recognise something else fun is happening.

A single mid pitch bark may mean that your dog is curious about a particular person, or situation, and they want to make contact. It may be linked to pleasure and excitement – Gus often does a single bark when he sees my mum, because he loves my mum. Possibly more than he loves me.

A string of solitary barks with deliberate pauses between each one - "woof," pause, "woof," pause, "woof," pause - is a sign of a lonely dog asking for companionship. For around two months last year I heard this bark for most of each weekday from a dog in a house just over the hill. I suspect the dog was left alone while the owners went to work, but the dog was not happy. Then one day the bark was heard no more. I often wonder what had changed. I just hope the dog, wherever it now is, is more relaxed and settled.

Aggressive barks are usually low-pitched and mixed with growls. People may describe a dog's aggressive barking as 'vicious', which is their shorthand description about the vocalisation and its intensity, duration, frequency and tone.

Finally, there is a bark which sounds something like "Harr-ruff". Your dog will produce this sound with their front legs flat on the ground and their rear end held high. It's an invitation bark, aimed at another dog or human and usually means "Let's play!" Or "Let's interact!"

There are many other types of barks, many similar to yips and whines: think of a puppy's plaintive bark when it's crying for its mother. This mix of alarm barks and distress barks is unique to domestic dogs.

Interestingly, we humans seem to have an innate response to dogs barking.

Studies have shown that humans, even non-dog owning ones, are actually very good at interpreting canine vocalisations and the emotional states behind them. People that were played the sounds of dogs barking in various contexts – such as when they were separated from their owners, or were barking in play - could tell the difference between them without having to see the dog itself.

Excessive barking

Excessive barking can be a problem in certain breeds such as the Finnish Spitz, some schnauzers and the guarding breeds, but any dog of any breed may exhibit problem barking. Just like some people talk incessantly, because they love the sound of their own voice, some dogs are similar.

But what is excessive barking? Well, it's in the ear of the beholder. Excessive barking (as defined by the Dog and Cat Management Act 1995) is 'when a dog creates a noise, by barking or otherwise, which persistently occurs or continues to such a degree or extent that it unreasonably interferes with the peace, comfort or convenience of a person.'

Barking is therefore excessive if someone thinks it is. Which is, of course, very subjective. Some people will complain about 'normal' barking, where a dog alerts to the postman or visitors, even when the dog quietens as soon as the visitor enters or the postman leaves.

What can you do to reduce barking?

I will look at specific problem barking areas in subsequent chapters, but what follows is some general advice. First a key point:

You cannot deal with barking if you are not present with the dog.

A person once rang me to ask to buy an anti-bark collar for her dog. She left her dog outside in her garden while she was at work and the neighbours had complained about the dog barking. She wanted a bark activated device: an audible alarm, citronella spray, or bark activated vibration or electric collar. I refused to help her obtain one. While anti-barking devices and collars may have a small effect in the short term, they are generally unpleasant to the dog and if they are not linked to any other training, they will lose their effect quite quickly - and may make the problem worse.

There's no magic bullet. Prevention and training are the only options.

1) Work out the why

First, work out why your dog is barking. Is it in response to someone or something passing by such as other dogs or strangers? Is it because the postman has arrived? Or to get your attention? The 'why' is important.

Perhaps you think your dog is barking because they are bored. If this is the case, the first step is to provide more exercise and especially mental stimulation. This will refocus your dog's mind onto something more positive and help tire them out.

2) Manage the situation

A key next step is management. Things such as:

- Avoid leaving your dog on guard by the front window or door. Keep them in a back room until the postman has been
- Never leave your dog outside on his own – it's too easy for them to develop a barking habit. Monitor your dog when they are out in the garden. Bring them back inside if they start to bark.
- Only give your dog attention when they are quiet
- Close blinds or curtains to prevent them monitoring passing traffic, people, other dogs, cats or birds

Verbal corrections such as saying "no", or shouting, or yelling at your dog, or any other form of punishment, can make barking worse. Instead, if you can anticipate a situation when your dog is likely to bark (such as someone walking past, or knocking at the door), you can teach them 'quiet'.

3) Teach 'quiet'

As soon as you hear even the smallest first woof, say "quiet". Help your dog understand by putting a treat under their nose. As soon as they stop barking, praise them well, then, after a couple of seconds of quiet, give them the treat. (Waiting that time means you can be sure you are rewarding the quiet rather than the barking.) Repeat three times, then try the cue and hand movement without the treat, producing the reward once your dog stops barking. You can also encourage your dog to run away from the door or window into the kitchen or other back room, to get their reward.

If your dog doesn't listen and continues to bark after you ask them to be quiet, IMMEDIATELY get up and leave the room, shutting the door. (Or put your dog behind a shut door if you are outside.) Wait until they have been quiet for 2-3 seconds then return and praise. Leave (or shut the door) again at once if barking restarts. Praise silence.

Alternatively, keep a house line on your dog so that you can use that to remove them away from the focus of their attention. The line is best, because picking your dog up or otherwise touching them to move them away can reward the barking behaviour.

4) Out and about

If barking occurs when you are out for a walk (for example, if your dog barks at other dogs or people) say "whoops," immediately turn sharply through 180 degrees and walk in the opposite direction. When your dog has been quiet for 2-3 seconds, praise, treat, and turn back to walk in the original direction, or in a new direction away from the barking trigger, if necessary.

Barking myths

Let's bust a few common myths about barking:

1) All barking dogs should be taught the 'quiet' cue

Not necessarily. For many nuisance barking problems teaching 'quiet' can be extremely useful, but it's often better to manage the trigger situation by avoiding it or removing the dog. And for barking related to aggression, teaching 'quiet' is most definitely not an appropriate option.

2) Deaf dogs don't bark

False. Excessive barking is actually more likely in deaf dogs. Deaf dogs are more likely to engage in behaviours they find self-stimulating, including excessive barking, excessive licking, spinning, and chewing inappropriate objects, than hearing dogs. Though some other unwanted behaviours, such as chasing rabbits and cats, and rolling in and eating poo, occur less frequently in deaf dogs than in hearing dogs.

3) Dogs bark and howl at the moon

False. Dogs howl for the same reasons their wild cousins do --

communication. Wolves howl, day or night, full moon or dark, to call to pack members separated from the pack, to let other packs know the boundaries of their territory, and sometimes just for the hell of it, like a community sing-song.

Dogs howl and bark to make contact with other dogs when they're bored or lonely, or when they hear another sound that resembles a howl: a siren, a human singing, or in Gus's case, my shower. The moon is completely irrelevant. The 'at the moon' part probably comes from the posture they assume - head back, nose to the sky -- which directs the sound up and out so that it carries over a wider area.

There are lots of other reasons dogs bark, many of which I'll cover in the next few chapters. But please seek professional help if you are struggling with your dog's barking.

Summary

- Barking is normal canine communication.
- Most dogs bark a few times then settle again quickly after the stimulus has stopped.
- Learn to recognise what your dog is communicating when they bark

If you are annoyed by your dog barking at every little thing then try the suggestions here and in the subsequent chapters. And of course, please seek professional help if you need.

Your dog will thank you - and less coffee will be spilt.

24

EXCITEMENT BARKING

"**W**oof-woof-woof-woof-woof-woof-woof-woof-woof-woof..." *Elaine felt her cheeks were aflame as she struggled to drag Buddy away. She had hoped this route would be quieter and there would be fewer dogs. Which there were - but Buddy had spotted a Labrador playing with their owner in the distance. And once Buddy spotted another dog that was it. He became almost uncontrollable, spinning on the lead and barking his head off. All Elaine could do was to try and get out of the situation as quickly as possible, dragging her errant Schnauzer behind her in desperation. Two walkers stared at her strangely and she wanted a large hole to open up and swallow her. Her dreams of pleasant, companionable ambles with Buddy were shattered by the reality that whenever he saw another dog he started barking and kept going until they were out of sight. And being at home wasn't much better. Buddy had a barking fit at anything that went past the window or any visitor that came to the door. Elaine was puzzled and frustrated. There was no nastiness in Buddy, he was very friendly to people and dogs. If only she could control his barking and get some peace and quiet.*

We talked in a previous chapter about whining in excitement. Perhaps you can cope with that - but what if your dog barks uncontrollably when excited, like Buddy?

Dogs who bark madly at other dogs, or postmen, or visitors, or passers-by, or whatever, are a common problem. These dogs tend to be easily aroused, the sort of dog who barks at any noise or disturbance. They are often excitable in other ways too, such as getting into a frenzy when playing, or spinning in excitement when you pick up the lead, or open the food cupboard door.

Often this noisy excitement can be exacerbated by you or your friends and family by giving your dog a huge fuss the second you come through the door, or encouraging jumping up, or continually playing arousing games such as fetch, or play wrestling with your pup.

Some of this is related to genetics and breed. Certain breeds are naturally more laid back, such as the Italian Spinone I once knew who would sleep nearly 23 hours a day if given the chance and never summoned up enough energy to bark at anything. Others are naturally more excitable. Gus is a good example. Even as a pup he only slept around twelve hours a day and he still alerts to every little noise and movement now, at nearly ten years old.

Happy or over-aroused

How can you tell if your dog is happy or over-aroused? Happy dogs will often have a wide mouthed grin, with their tongue hanging out. But if that appearance is also linked with them panting excessively, barking a lot, pacing around and being unable to settle down, then your dog is probably over-aroused.

Over-arousal can be shown in other ways - your dog freezing and becoming fixated on another dog, or that favourite tennis ball. These dogs may show excessive friendliness, jumping up, and mouthing and biting at clothes or hands. They find it difficult to focus and will often snatch an offered treat rather than taking it nicely. Male dogs may show their 'lipstick', that is, the top of their penis may protrude, and they may show excessive mounting behaviour.

There's nothing nasty about these 'naughty but nice' dogs, but they are always getting into trouble and annoying their owners with their behaviour and they find it difficult to calm down and control themselves.

Over-arousal is a form of stress called eustress, which we talked briefly about at the start of the book. This is positive stress but with some potentially negative implications.

Think of how you felt when you bought your first house, or got married, or had your first child. Or imagine how you would feel if you won the lottery. These are all highly exciting situations for you - and your dog is feeling and responding in the same way to the things that excite them. That cat on the fence; the doorbell; seeing another dog; children running around; you coming back home;

playing; all these things can trigger pleasure - and excitement barking.

Every dog has a normal-for-them baseline character and level of excitement which can vary hugely even within dogs of the same breed. Dogs who spend some time every day being over-excited and barking at passers by, chasing balls or generally getting up to nonsense, will gradually reset their excitability (arousal) baseline higher and higher, meaning they find it easier and easier to becoming excited and bark - and more and more difficult to become, and stay, calm.

For their sake, and your sanity, it's worth doing something about it.

What to do about excitement barking

Whatever you do it's unlikely you'll be able to stop your dog barking completely, but you can modify the barking to an acceptable or at least bearable level.

My initial recommendation, as always, is to take your dog for a check up with your vet, as any seemingly extreme behaviour can be exacerbated by an underlying medical condition.

Assuming there is nothing medically wrong, here are some tips to help you control your excited mutt. This training needs a calm approach - and bucket loads of patience.

1) Check the basics

Make sure your dog is getting sufficient exercise and is not being left alone for long periods. These things can create chronic stress, which is also a cause of excitement barking. Walks need to provide both physical and mental exercise for your dog, so include plenty of sniff time.

If you have to leave your dog alone for long periods because you have to go to work, then arrange for a neighbour, dog walker or friend to pop in and provide some company and play for your dog and break up the monotony of your absence.

2) Don't encourage the barking

Make sure you are not adding to, or perpetuating, the barking. No shouting "Shut UP!" in frustration, difficult though this may be, I know. No chatting away, "There, there, Buddy, there's no need to get so excited, just calm down"; no repeating words in a gradually increasing tone "quiet, Quiet, QUIET!" Your admonitions simply become background noise, or worse, your dog thinks you are joining in and feels encouraged to continue their noisy behaviour.

3) Keep all interactions with your dog low key

Project a calm, serene manner when returning home, when greeting your dog, and when giving them a fuss. An excited voice, ruffling hand touches, frequent exclamations and breathy, staccato chat will make any dog more excited and will trigger barking in your excitable canine. Talk in a lower, slower voice, stroke rather than ruffle, and make movements more deliberate. Every few minutes calmly ask your dog to perform a behaviour they know well - sit, down, roll over, fetch something, or whatever. This will help keep them in 'thinking' mode rather than their usual excitable, reactive state.

4) Use hand signals

It may help to use hand signals rather than verbal cues with excitable dogs. Dogs often respond more readily to a physical cue, such as a hand movement or change of body position, than to spoken cues. And if they are barking, they may not hear your spoken cue anyway.

For example, when asking for quiet, teach the cue of a finger across your lips in that age old way, or teach your dog to stop still using a hand held out like a policeman. These cues need to be taught like any other cue - by linking the action to the behaviour you want - but once taught, your excitedly barking dog will often respond much better to these cues.

5) Garner patience

If your dog barks to get something they want, such as to go outside, simply stand still and wait. Once your dog is quiet -

perhaps because they stop barking to wonder what you are doing - praise gently then let them outside.

Teach and practice other games requiring self-control, such as leave it, walking nicely on lead and doorway manners. (You can find all these and more in our Perfect Pet online course at online. downdog.co.uk)

6) Deal with trigger points

For those dogs who break into a fusillade of barking at a particular trigger, such as the doorbell, the postman, or whatever, there is more specific advice in the later chapters in this book. For now, here are some general points to help:

- For barking while you are talking to someone at the door, or when out on a walk, give your dog a toy to carry or something to chew. Holding or chewing keeps your dog's mouth busy and chewing is calming - and it's difficult to bark with your mouth full.

- If seeing other dogs is one of your dogs barking triggers, practice calm behaviour with other dogs by finding a dog-owning friend or helpful neighbour with a laid back, calm dog. Go for walks together, walking side by side and rewarding your dog for ignoring the other dog and paying any attention to you. Walking groups often have one or two dogs around as well, so finding a local group might be another option.

- Another way to help your dog-excitable hound is to find places where dogs congregate, at commons or beaches, or outside the dreaded dog parks, or near local pet shops. Find a place to sit and watch a short distance away and reward your dog for any and all calm, quiet behaviour.

We taught Elaine how to keep Buddy calmer using the methods above plus some specific work on reducing his arousal around other dogs. He became a sniff game addict, was far calmer in the house, and he and Elaine were able to enjoy their walks together as she'd always wanted.

Summary

- Barking in excitement is related to over-arousal
- Make sure you are not perpetuating and encouraging the barking
- Training is about helping your dog learn to control themselves better

In the next few chapters we'll look at some other common barking issues and what to do about them. First, I'll address an annoying problem, barking for attention.

25

BARKING FOR ATTENTION

"**P**lease help. My daughter lives abroad so my only affordable way to speak to her is via Skype. But our conversations are ruined by my dog, Freya. As soon as I sit down and open the computer, she starts yipping away and trying to jump on my lap. I thought she was getting excited when she heard my daughter's voice, so I tried letting her see the screen, but it makes no difference. I've tried shutting her out of the room but she damaged the door with her scratching and she added barking to her yipping! I don't know what else to do. I just want to talk to my daughter in peace."

This heartfelt query came in recently from Sarah about her dog, miniature schnauzer Freya.

It's no fun being pestered and assaulted both physically and aurally by annoying, high-pitched and very loud squeaks when you're trying to Skype call with your daughter in New Zealand, or talk to a friend on the phone. Some dogs will bark whenever the phone rings, and continue to bark until the phone call ends, which is equally annoying.

Others will determinedly paw at your legs, body or arms. One of our other clients, Mandy, had scratches all over her arms from her dog, Buddy. Buddy is a 2 year old Labrador cross, as goofy as anything and lovely, but he can be clumsy and, oh boy, he can be persistent. As a puppy, the family thought Buddy lifting a paw was cute so they encouraged 'give a paw'. But it started getting out of hand. If Mandy ignored Buddy's pawing, he started barking at her and mouthing her, as well as pawing at her.

So why do dogs like Freya and Buddy do these sorts of behaviours?

Very simply, for attention.

Dogs love our attention and will try all sorts of things to get and keep it. Who doesn't secretly love it when your pooch pushes their hard bony head under your arm demanding fuss? And if what they try works, and they get the attention they crave, through you looking at them, speaking to them or touching them, they'll keep doing it.

When you answer or call someone on a phone, or when you're Skyping or Face-timing friends or relatives, your dog knows that you're about to take attention away from them. Some will try almost anything to get that attention back.

One dog I knew used to run to the door, pretending she needed to go out to eliminate - something guaranteed to get attention. Another crafty canine used to attack a cushion, growling and shaking at it. (That family went through quite a lot of cushions before they sought our help. I'm glad to say their cushions are now safe.) Dogs can be pretty creative in finding ways to demand our attention.

Gus sometimes barks or paws at me when he wants something, and also if he's bored. Most times I'll look at him and ask "What do you want?" - so the behaviour works. The fact that it doesn't work every time actually increases the likelihood of him repeating the behaviour, because dogs are gamblers at heart.

As a normal human being, you'll find it really difficult to ignore your dog barking, jumping up, pawing at your flesh, ripping your clothing, or squeaking a toy in your ear. So you inevitably give your dog attention - usually by yelling at them to "Shut up", "Be quiet!", "Stop it", or, my own favourite, "Lie down." Or you might persist in pushing them down if they jump up. Perhaps you glare at them, while you abortively flap your hands at them to signal them to go away. And you watch them closely, concerned at what their next move might be.

"Hurrah" says your dog, "that worked."

And so these behaviours continue.

So what can you do about it?

How to deal with barking for attention

Barking for attention can be difficult to change because it has worked so well for your dog until now. All attention seeking behaviours, once established, take a bucketload of time and patience to deal with.

After all, your dog wouldn't bark or paw if those behaviours didn't work for them. Dogs do the things they get rewarded for.

Imagine I gave you £5 every time you clapped three times. I did this for several weeks, so you came to expect the £5 for clapping three times. If I suddenly stopped giving you the money, would you simply stop clapping? No. You would almost certainly try again, many times, probably getting closer to me and even clapping in my face and you'd persist until it became clear that clapping wasn't paying any more.

But then I pick up my purse. You first instinct would be to clap again, as this time the clapping might finally work to get you some money. And if I then gave you £5 for clapping, you would definitely keep trying and you'd clap any time you thought there might be a chance of getting your reward.

Now this is quite a silly example, but I hope it makes the point that behaviours that work get repeated. The clapping will return any time a reward looks possible - and will return in abundance if the behaviour occasionally gets a reward.

Can you see how your dog will feel and act the same about attention seeking behaviours such as barking or pawing at you?

The simple answer to the barking or pawing is to stop giving your dog any attention for the unwanted behaviour. Simple - but it requires patience and persistence; in particular, being more persistent than your dog. And if the barking or other obnoxious behaviour has become a habit, simply ignoring may never stop it.

Here are some tips to reduce unwanted attention barking:

1) Make sure your dog is getting sufficient exercise and stimulation

Not just physical exercise - mindless ball chasing encourages fitness, which leads to more mindless ball chasing - but plenty of mental exercise, especially walks and games that get your dog using their nose.

Play 'find it' for treats or toys on walks, lay out a scent trail for your dog and play hide and seek - there are plenty of games you can play to encourage your dog to use their nose. Sniffing is exhausting for dogs and tires them out beautifully.

2) Provide an alternative

When you are going to make a Skype or Facetime call, you could simply go into another room and leave your dog shut in elsewhere. If, like Freya, they create even more disturbance by scratching at the door, teach them that being in that room on their own is wonderful, by giving them a long lasting chew, filled Kong, a lickimat, or other similar food toy whenever they are in that room.

3) Train a specific phone behaviour

If your dog barks when you answer a ringing phone, settling your dog elsewhere is not always the answer, because phone calls are rarely planned. They are irregular and occasional - so dealing with this problem means you need to train your dog to react differently in response to the ringing.

Here's how:

- Either record your phone ringing or use a second phone to ring your usual phone
- Sit with your dog, have some treats ready
- Play one ring only then stop
- Praise and treat all quiet behaviour
- Repeat - many times, gradually adding more rings
- Once your dog stops barking at the ring tone, pretend to answer the phone, continuing to reward your dog for all quiet behaviour

Teaching your dog to lie down by your feet while you chat on the phone works well. You just need to make sure manna (rewards) continues to rain from above while they remain lying down quietly. Which means you needs to be prepared and always have some treats on you ready for unexpected calls. It's not a quick fix, but with practice, they'll happily lie down and chomp away while you natter.

Or you could run to a particular place, a bed or mat, when you play your phone ring, and give your dog a reward there. This will teach your dog that in response to the phone ringing they should run to their place where they'll get a yummy reward. But you need to make this easy as you'll need to do it every time you get a phone call which can be difficult.

Phones have a habit of ringing at odd times, such as when you're in the bedroom sorting laundry, in the kitchen cooking, refereeing your children's fight, or on the loo. You may need to train your dog to run to their place in all these different situations - and more. Which can be difficult, time-consuming - and can seem never-ending. However, it can work well.

For some dogs it may be that a certain ring tone that causes them to react, so changing your ring tone may help, especially if you train your dog from the start to perform a particular behaviour when that tone sounds.

Just make sure you are rewarding the behaviour you want rather than the previous obnoxious attention seeking behaviour.

4) Other types of barking for attention

If your dog is barking at other times for attention, you have two options.

The first is to ignore the barking and never (and I mean NEVER) respond to it. Everyone in your family needs to be consistent too. Eventually the behaviour will die out because behaviours that don't get a reward aren't worth doing.

But this can take a very long time. To help this process, focus on trying to reward your dog when they are NOT barking and try to reward every time they look at you. Looking will gradually become their default 'want-attention' behaviour instead of barking. It's up to you to watch for the look and reward it. This option works particularly well for dogs who paw for attention - as long as you remember to notice and reward every look.

Gus has this down to a fine art. He walks over to me and stands sideways on to me, with an intent gaze focused on my face. He is careful to stand in my line of sight and he is impossible to ignore - the behaviour works. And I much prefer it to pawing or barking, so I continue to reward it.

The second option is to teach your dog to do something else instead. Perhaps ask for a sit, or a down, before giving them attention. Just make sure you notice what they're doing or they may quickly revert to barking or pawing again.

Freya quickly learnt to lie down by Sarah's feet and chomp on a filled Kong while Sarah was on Skype and Sarah can now enjoy long chats with her daughter.

Mandy is still working on teaching Buddy not to use his paws so enthusiastically. Buddy will now look before pawing and as long as Mandy notices that she can reward it and prevent her arms suffering any more. Unfortunately the rest of her family aren't being as helpful as they could be, which is why it is taking some time, but she'll get there eventually.

Summary

- Dogs repeat behaviours that result in attention from their owner
- Management is a key element for certain barking triggers
- Focusing on rewarding quiet behaviour will reduce attention barking

Of course, many barks have a greater purpose than simply gaining your attention. We'll look at the most common of these, barking at the postman or other deliveries, in the next chapter.

26

BARKING AT THE POSTMAN

M*ax took his self-appointed job as protector of the home and his people very seriously. Anyone approaching the house was subjected to a loud fusillade of sharp, staccato barks, increasing in volume and ferocity if the person continued to approach. His owner, Nick, kept the front door locked as he was terrified Max would bite someone, he barked so viciously. Out walking Max one day, Nick saw his postman coming out of a neighbouring house, so he stopped, thinking that it might be a good idea if Max said hello to him. But the dog's barking and growling got worse, and Nick was afraid Max might actually bite. Sensibly, he backed off.*

Does your dog hate your postman?

Does he launch into a barking frenzy as the mail drops on the mat?

There's a house I walk past on one of my regular walks in which lives a cockapoo who barks ferociously and frenziedly when we walk past and hurls itself at the glazed front window. The window flexes and rebounds repeatedly and I fear that eventually that dog will crash through. Luckily there is a wall and closed gate if it did ever happen to keep passers-by safe. Though I'd hate to be their postman.

Perhaps you are thankful for your double glazing and well-fixed frames, otherwise your pooch would be through the window and shredding your postman's trousers.

It's no fun for the postman either. Royal Mail reports around 2,500 dog attacks on postmen and women (post-people?) each year. Around 80% of attacks occur at the front door, in the garden or in the street just outside the house. Our postcode across Northern Ireland, BT, had the most attacks recorded of any other postcode in the UK in 2019-2020, 20% more than the next worst postcode.

Royal Mail will prosecute owners for dogs that bite if the police do not, or cannot, take appropriate action. And you should know that Royal Mail can refuse to deliver your mail if they feel there is a significant risk of a dog attack or bite.

So why do so many dogs react so crazily to postmen?

Well there are several reasons. The first reason is that this is normal dog behaviour. Your dog may simply be protecting their territory. Most breeds develop some protective instinct around their home once they reach adolescence, especially the guarding breeds. They start to bark if anyone comes to the door to warn you about a possible problem and to warn off intruders. Most of us appreciate this - as long as it doesn't get out of hand or become excessive.

The second reason is - it works. The postman comes, your dog barks and the postman goes away. Success! The dog has no idea the postman was going to leave anyway - your dog may believe it was his barking that made the postman go away.

Thirdly, postmen come back. Despite your dog's success in making the postman go away yesterday, they came back again today - much to your dog's annoyance. So your dog thinks he'll have to try even harder today - and that frustration and repetition means the reaction often becomes more severe over time.

Your dog could be a self-created addict. When dogs experience a sudden, strong emotion, their body reacts by producing a flood of chemicals, including adrenaline and noradrenaline, the fight or flight hormones, and it takes a long time for these changes to subside. Some dogs can become addicted to the feelings they get from this chemical soup and so they enjoy practising their barking even more. These are the dogs who stay glued to the window at the time the postman usually comes and can't be easily distracted from their vigil.

The fifth reason is habit. Anything, if repeated regularly, can become a habit. Because postmen come most days, your dog gets a lot of practice at barking at them and it's easy for this to become a habit.

The final, sixth reason is more subtle. Your dog may bark because they have generalised from a previous scary or annoying experience. Perhaps your dog reacted by barking at a delivery man who frightened him; from a loud bang when they dropped the postbox lid or a parcel or whatever; or a sudden unexpected knock on the door. Or maybe the post itself scared your dog - the shock of it coming through the door. Your dog may then generalise the scary experience and learn to bark at postmen, and any other delivery person, in anticipation of some frightening event or noise.

Whatever the cause, barking at postmen or deliveries is a common problem.

So what can you do about it?

How to keep postmen and other delivery people safe

Your number one concern is not how to deal with your dog, but must be your postman and delivery driver's safety. Make sure you are not included in the awful Royal Mail dog attack statistics. Prevention is vital.

Never leave your dog outside when the postman might come. If you are outside with your dog when the postman or a delivery might arrive, make sure your dog is safely on lead. If you have a rear garden, make sure there is a securely fastened, and preferably locked, side gate. If you cannot ensure your dog can be kept away from your front drive or gate, install a mail or parcel box just outside your property instead.

Protect your mail and parcels as well as your postman. Think about putting a mailbox on the wall of your house, or attach a wire basket to catch your mail inside the door, rather than having the mail pushed through the letter box to land on the floor. This is essential if your dog tends to attack and destroy the mail as it arrives. It can also protect your postman from nips to their fingers as they push the mail through the door. In September 2020, the High Court ruled that dog owners who fail to take steps to prevent their dogs from biting postal workers' fingers through a letter box, whether the owners are home or not, could be convicted of an offence under the Dangerous Dogs Act in the UK.

If you need to open your door to sign for a delivery, or receive a large parcel, make sure your dog is shut away securely in a back room or behind a baby gate or other barrier before you open the door. Teach your children not to open the door until you are there - dogs can easily push past children.

Wait several minutes before allowing your dog out after the postman or a delivery has been, otherwise your dog may hurl themselves at the door in a barking frenzy. This is not a behaviour that protects your fixtures and fittings - and it risks your dog injuring themselves, too.

Finally, be careful when arriving back home after a trip out. Check there is no postman (or anyone else) in view before letting your dog out of your car and always use a lead, even for the few steps from your car into your home.

How to stop your dog barking at deliveries

Here are a few tips on what you can do to reduce your dog's barking:

1) Start training early

Let your new puppy meet the postman each day. If the postman is happy to do so, ask them to give your puppy a treat each time they come. Unfortunately, most people don't do this for long enough - it needs to be for several weeks or even months. And it can be difficult to catch your postman every day: they are busy people with a job to do, after all. But it should be an essential part of your puppy's training.

2) Create a happy, positive link in your dog's mind

This can be as easy as simply giving your dog a few really yummy treats as the postman approaches your home. Up the number you give as the postman delivers the mail, then gradually drop off the treats as the postman leaves. If you do this every day, or at least as often as you can, several times a week, your dog will then learn to look forward to the postman coming and focus on getting their reward rather than barking their head off.

This can be more difficult to do with deliveries as they are not as predictable. Keep a pot of treats handy near the front door or in the room where your dog keeps watch so you can grab them to do this training when you hear someone approaching.

3) Prevent your dog having the opportunity to bark

Shut your dog out of front rooms and keep them away from front windows, hallways and doors. This is the easiest method to use and it has the major benefit of preventing your dog practising (and getting better and better at) the behaviour.

We worked with Nick and Max to implement a safety first policy of keeping Max away from the front of the house during the day. Nick worked hard on helping Max see the post and deliveries as fun times using treats as described above. This has reduced Max's frantic barking to more reasonable, normal levels. Now they can walk past their postman in the street with no reaction from Max, though the management policy of not allowing Max near the front of the house will remain for some time yet, perhaps permanently.

Summary

- Dog attacks on postmen are sadly common and can result in you not having your mail delivered
- Behaviours that are practiced get stronger
- Safety is the number one priority

Barking at the postman is closely linked with barking at the doorbell generally, which we'll look at in more detail in the next chapter.

27

BARKING AT THE DOORBELL

D*ing-dong, ding-dong.* "Woof-woof-woof-woof-woof-woof-woof-woof...." *Johnny sighed deeply. Baby Susannah was just about to drop off to sleep and he had been longing for a few minutes respite after an hour of constant grizzling and pacing around consoling her. The gentle music of the doorbell hadn't disturbed her, but Dino's barking had. With a heavy heart, Johnny picked up the now screeching baby and set off back downstairs. The barking got louder and louder as they descended. "Shut UP, Dino," snarled Johnny, with no real hope of the dog responding. Indeed, that was the case and Johnny spent a difficult minute trying to fend Dino away with his leg while keeping hold of screaming Susannah and, with his third hand, opening the door to a now impatient delivery driver.*

Deliveries and visitors nearly always arrive at inopportune moments, don't they? It's beyond the scope of this book to explore why that is, but suffice to say, unexpected door knocks and the subsequent fusillade of barking from your dog has been the cause of many a crying child, disarrayed drink, and hammering heart.

We live a mile away from the sea, which results in our doorbell dying fairly regularly due to the salty air. Our doorbell is not something we test every week, although we probably should, so it's only when someone comes to the door that we realise it is no longer working. At those times, Gus's warning of a delivery is very welcome, because if I'm in the kitchen, I can't hear a visitor knocking.

One of the comforting reasons for owning a dog, apart from furry cuddles, is the feeling of protection that comes from your watch-dog barking when people come. It adds to a feeling of safety, especially if you live alone - and having a dog has been proven to reduce the risk of burglary.

But barking at the doorbell can also be an annoying habit, especially if your dog doesn't shut up after a few barks. There's nothing worse than struggling to communicate with a visitor through a barrage of barking.

Why dogs bark at doorbells

As they grow, the majority of dogs will develop some territorial awareness and begin to respond with different vocalisations when someone or something invades their space - which includes barking at the doorbell as a warning that someone has come to your home. But dogs can bark at the doorbell for any number of other reasons.

Some dogs bark because they are excited at the prospect of a new person visiting.

Others might bark because they are anxious about new people coming into your home.

For some dogs it becomes a learnt behaviour. They equate their barking with you opening the door, so they imagine they are training you to open the door in response to their bark.

Or it may be an association with your behaviour. If someone ringing the doorbell always stirs you into action and you get up and walk towards the door, your dog will may bark in anticipation of your movement.

This behaviour may not be a particular problem for you. It isn't for me - Gus does a short volley of alert barks then shuts up to wait to see what will happen. I like this behaviour, mainly because it lets us know someone has come when the doorbell isn't working, so I'm happy to let it continue. And I make sure it will by thanking and rewarding Gus when he lets me know someone is there

But if your dog's barking at the doorbell is a problem for you, perhaps because you don't want it to disturb your sleeping baby, then here are a few tips to help.

How to control doorbell barking

It is unrealistic to expect your dog never to bark at a stranger approaching your home. Most dogs develop some level of territorial guarding behaviour as they enter maturity, usually between 8 and 14 months of age and, without any direct training from you, they will start to bark when someone comes to the house.

You probably don't want to prevent this behaviour, after all, it is a comforting warning - but you may want to control and manage it so that it doesn't become excessive. Try to encourage and teach your dog what you want them to do as early as possible. Here are two suggestions:

1) Gain control of the barking

If your dog quickly quietens after the first few barks as you move to answer the door, the easiest way to gain control of their barking is to teach them to be quiet on cue. Here's how:

- Thank your dog for telling you someone has arrived - that's only polite, after all.
- Then praise the not-barking for two seconds. The easiest way to do this is to say, "Thank you. Good quiet one, good quiet two," then give your dog a treat.
- With repetition, your dog will learn to shut up as soon as you say "thank you," in anticipation of their reward.

For many dogs this is the simple, easy and quick solution.

2) Teach a specific behaviour

Another option is to teach your dog to go to a 'place', such as a bed or a special mat, once they have alerted you to the visitor. Where this place is, is up to you and will depend to a large extent on the layout of your house. Usual 'places' are a corner of your hallway, or under the stairs, or in a room at the rear of your home. For many people a good 'place' to use is the kitchen or another back room. This has the added advantage that you can shut your dog in that room while you deal with any visitor.

To teach this behaviour, the best way is to involve a friend or family member to ring your doorbell while you teach your dog what you want. If no-one is available, another option is to record the sound of your doorbell on your phone so you can play it during training sessions.

Here's how to train 'place':

- At the ring of the doorbell, your dog may or may not bark - they will have seen your set-up anyway and realise something is different. It doesn't matter if they don't bark, you are using the sound of the doorbell as the predicting cue, so whether they bark or not isn't important
- Once the bell has rung, give your cue ("bed" or "place" or whatever) in an excited voice, run to the place or bed and wait for your dog to join you
- Praise your dog well and give them 2 or 3 treats one after the other on their bed or place
- Repeat, many times
- You should find your dog starting to anticipate, so after each doorbell ring they'll run to the bed / place and wait expectantly for their reward

Many people stop there, but this is only the start of the training. The next stages take the most time.

Practice asking your dog to go to their place when you are in different places and positions in your house - when you are sitting down, or in the kitchen, or upstairs, because you never know where you'll be when the doorbell rings for real.

Next, make the practice unexpected. Send a friend or family member outside and ask them to wait several minutes before ringing the bell. In the meantime, you need to pretend you are doing whatever you'd normally do - washing up, sitting at your desk, ironing, reading, or whatever. As soon as the doorbell rings it's likely your dog will bark. Say "Thank you," then give your bed / place cue and go with your dog there to reward them.

The final stage is to teach your dog to remain in their bed or place while you deal with the visitor. The easiest way to teach your dog to stay in their place or bed is to give them a long lasting chew such as a Kong or lickimat. It's a good idea to have a Kong or lickimat ready prepared in the fridge each day so you always have something to hand. And if there aren't any visitors that day, your dog can have the food toy as a special evening treat.

Make sure to follow this routine every time your doorbell rings. And that's more about training yourself to remember to thank your dog and send them to their place every time. Which may prove to be the hardest part of the training.

For many people, their dog barking at the doorbell is a useful part of dog ownership. But it's worth doing some training to prevent a future problem - especially if you are planning to have a small baby. Johnny and his partner trained Dino to 'go to bed' in their kitchen and visitors and deliveries could be then dealt with in peace. We didn't have as much success in teaching baby Susannah not to cry.

Summary

- Doorbell barking can results from several causes
- Managing and controlling the barking is important for your and your visitors' sanity
- Teach your dog an alternative, acceptable behaviour instead

More of a problem can be dogs who bark at things passing by your home, which we'll look at in the next chapter.

28

BARKING AT PASSING, MOVING THINGS

argaret was relaxing in her comfy armchair when a "Woof,
Woof, Woof, Woof, Woof" almost made her drop her book.
Her heart thudding madly, she glared at her cockapoo, who
was standing erect on the back of the sofa by the window, gaze fixed at the
van across the road. Why did Tilly have to bark at everything and anything
that went past? It didn't matter if it was a child and their parent walking
to school, a car or van pulling up nearby, or the postman - although the
latter did get an especially loud and prolonged bark. Tilly spent most of her
time standing up against, or even on, the back of the sofa, watching what
was going on outside. And she always let Margaret know when something
was happening. Margaret sighed and picked up her book, hoping to at least
finish a chapter before the next interruption.

It's common for people to ask me for help because their dog barks excessively at people, dogs and things going past the home.

As we discussed in the previous chapter, it's normal for dogs to bark at people coming to your home, especially postmen. They are giving a warning – to let you know there's something there. Most dogs develop some level of territorial guarding as they reach maturity, around a year old for most. This behaviour develops naturally and shows itself as barking to tell you someone has arrived at your home.

As mentioned in the last chapter, Gus will usually bark a few times as a timely notification that someone has arrived. I say "thank you" then Gus wanders off, having done his job, and I deal with the visitor.

For most dog owners that type of behaviour is a boon, not a problem. But constant barking at things going past your home can be a huge difficulty.

Some breeds are more prone to barking at people, vehicles, dogs or cats going past your home than others, especially the guarding and herding breeds, highly territorial dogs, and those stimulated by movement. And if your dog, like Tilly, barks at anything and everything that passes by your home, then the barking can quickly become an annoying problem.

The cause is not always simple territorial barking.

Many dogs develop a habit of barking at things going past as a form of self-recreation, sometimes to an almost obsessive level. A front room window or glass door often acts as a fascinating wide screen TV for your dog. Passing things moving across their 'screen' excite them, so they bark.

Yet more dogs might develop the behaviour as an outlet for boredom. Boredom in dogs is a significant problem. Dogs can't read books or watch TV, so dogs with little to do will find ways to entertain themselves, which often involves barking at people, dogs, cats and cars going past the home.

Both bored dogs and those looking for stimulation will find places to settle themselves, such as by a glass front door or on the back of a chair or settee by a front window, or even a windowsill. They may spend the majority of their day there, barking regularly.

What to do about it

What can you do about barking at the front window or front door? There are three main options to try. The first uses management, the second focusses on you, and the third is around training an alternative behaviour.

1) Prevent access

This is the simplest solution. Stopping access to their barking spot at the front of your home will prevent your dog practising the behaviour - practice makes perfect, after all. Here are a few options:

- Prevent access by closing the front room door, or putting a barrier such as a baby gate across doorways or across the hallway
- Move any chair, sofa or table your dog uses as their watchtower away from the window

- Block windowsills with objects to prevent your dog jumping up to look out. Be careful if using plants to block access though - cleaning soil debris from carpets is a prolonged and thankless task. Ask me how I know…
- For large windows, large dogs, or open plan houses, you can 'change the picture' the dog can see by putting frosted film (available from DIY stores) over the lower part of your window. This allows light in but stops your dog seeing out clearly and works well in many cases. And it's easily removed whenever you want a clear view, or when you plan to move house

Last year we went to see a dog who was over-excited in the home and had started nipping the owners. After a little detective work, we discovered that this behaviour was worse just after he had barked at someone walking past their large front window. We suggested frosted window film to prevent him seeing passers-by walking past. At the next visit the nipping problem had disappeared, the dog was far calmer and the owners were delighted with such a simple solution.

2) Exercise your dog

If you suspect the behaviour may be due to boredom, sadly a common problem, make sure your dog is getting sufficient physical exercise and, especially, mental stimulation.

This includes regular (as a minimum, daily) walks which allow plenty of sniffing as well as physical movement. Your walk can involve a limited amount of chasing balls, but better games are finding hidden toys, playing hide and seek, or following a track or trail. Gus's favourite walk game is to find a hidden tennis ball or treat. Throwing balls and encouraging chasing usually makes dogs over-aroused (and super fit) rather than tiring them out, which can increase a barking problem.

A good option to help tire and calm your dog is to use your walks to do some basic training. Try asking for a behaviour such as sit, down or wait every 30-50 yards (metres) or so, or practice your loose lead walking games in intensive, short bursts. Practice recalls in safe areas off lead, or on a long line.

Most importantly, make sure your dog is getting enough mental exercise through training, sniff games and feeding in fun ways at home. Ditching the food bowl means dogs can satisfy their scavenging instinct by searching for food in snuffle mats, Kongs and other food toys, or through searching for hidden caches of their food around the home and garden.

Teach your dog to help you with some household chores, and teach them to help with husbandry and grooming procedures. For example, Gus, among other things, fetches dirty washing for me to put in the washing machine, fetches my slippers and carries cleaning cloths. He lifts each paw on cue to be cleaned and dried, opens his mouth for his teeth to be cleaned and checked, and places his head pointing upwards for kennel cough nasal drops.

Or do some fun trick training. Gus performs a range of tricks such as crossing his paws, acting shy, dropping dead, spinning, turning, wrapping his paws around things and so on. There are plenty of books available to give you ideas for trick training.

If your dog is mentally and physically tired they are then far more likely to snooze on the settee rather than hang over the back and bark at things going past.

I'll digress a little here, with a story about my sloppy trick training and a warning about making sure you are training what you mean to. I made the mistake of playing "show me" far too frequently with Gus, a game where I say that cue, then wait to see what behaviour he offers in the hope of him offering something new. He'll then cycle through his range of tricks, trying different things until I praise something. He subsequently started performing a cycle of tricks whenever he thought I wanted something - and now he'll sometimes cycle through those behaviours when I've actually asked for something else. Or when he knows I have treats on me and he decides he wants one. Silly me. This means I now have to work hard on proofing all my cues individually - making sure he does the behaviour requested, and only that behaviour.

Anyway, back to helping your front of house barking dog...

3) Teach your dog to stay calm

Teaching your dog to be calm as people, dogs and things go past is best taught before your dog develops their barking habit. Once your dog has settled into a barking routine, this training is prolonged and much more difficult - prevention and management as in the first point above are the better answers for such dogs.

Start this training by watching your dog to see what excites them most. Is it people, other dogs, cats, birds, bicycles, motorbikes, cars, tractors or lorries? Is it only when things are close by your home, or does the barking occur at anything that passes within sight?

Go with your dog to their 'watching' area when they are calm, at a quieter time of day. Sit or stand next to them. Wait for a passer by or something to drive past (or get a friend to help and tell them to walk by.) As soon as your dog notices the person or thing, chat to your dog happily, praise them well and give them a nice treat for staying calm and quiet. Repeat this many times until your dog gets the idea.

If your dog barks, immediately take them out of the room for several minutes until they are quiet and calm again.

Gradually work up to doing this training at busier times of day, such as early mornings or late afternoons when more people, dogs and cars will be moving across your dog's field of vision, going to and coming home from work and school. Vary where you are - with the dog, sitting down, moving around, dusting if you must, staying inside or outside the room or area, and so on. Just make sure you can see your dog so that you can go to them and reward all calm behaviour whenever they see someone or something outside.

If your dog struggles to remain calm, then work out why. Is it at busier times? Is it a particular noise? Or a particular type or speed of vehicle? Gus gets most unsettled by loud motorbikes going past at speed, for example.

Can you arrange for your dog to be in another part of the house at certain times? School run times, where there are many passers by and more cars, might be too much for your dog, so they are better kept away from their wide-screen TV windows at those times.

Putting effort into this training with a new dog or puppy can prevent a barking problem. With puppies, make sure you redouble your efforts at this training in adolescence when they start to develop their territorial guarding behaviour.

Margaret had an open plan house, so blocking access to the front window was not an option, but she was able to rearrange the furniture to make it more difficult for Tilly to find a vantage point. The things she found worked to minimise Tilly's barking were encouraging more sniffing on her walks and ditching the food bowl, instead, feeding in food toys. Tilly will now lie down and snooze rather than spend her time on alert watching the world go by.

Summary

- Barking at people and things passing your home is a common problem
- Prevention is the best way to control such barking
- Dogs who are physically satisfied and mentally tired are less likely to develop a problem barking habit

The above deals with this common form of barking in the home. But what about dogs who bark in the car? We'll talk about that in the next chapter.

29

BARKING IN THE CAR

G us's eyes lit up and his ears pricked even more than usual as I picked up the car keys. He just loves going out in the car. But it's an ongoing struggle to keep him calm. He's an excitable dog generally and, because he's a collie, is triggered by movement. At home he'll bark at Himself walking past my study window, or at sudden noises, or cats going past, or cars and delivery vans arriving. In the car, he barks principally when vehicles come up close behind, especially noisy ones such as motorbikes, or when they are towing a trailer, or when cars pass close at the side, when they or we are overtaking or turning, or we are squeezing through a narrow gap. It's something I didn't address properly when he was a puppy and it has continued to be a problem.

Those shrill yaps and barks from the backseat can be your dog expressing many emotions, from fear and frustration to exuberant joy. This barking can all sound similar - and the headache the noises produce is also the same. But what you do about it depends on the reason for the outbursts.

So how can you tell why your dog is barking in the car? Let's examine some clues.

There are three common reasons for barking in the car. If your pooch is normally fairly laid back but bursts into a cacophony of barking as soon as your car starts to move, the barking is likely to be a result of excitement and anticipation of what the car ride might mean - a lovely walk on a beach or the woods, or visiting friends. Very quickly, the barking habit generalises to every car journey - because your dog anticipates something wonderful every time.

Car barking may also be caused by anxiety. Sometimes it can be difficult to decide whether your dog is experiencing excitement or anxiety. And if you're driving, you can't (and shouldn't) turn round and see what your dog's body language is telling you. Some dogs may have had a scary event they linked with the car in the past and so now they have a negative, anxious association with the vehicle.

When you first get a new puppy, their early car rides can be traumatic - leaving the only home they have ever known or being taken to scary places such as the vet or groomer, where, to make things worse, nasty things might happen such as having sharp needle pricks or hearing noisy dryers. It's no wonder some dogs then become anxious about car journeys.

The third common reason for barking in the car is frustration. Barking in the car is often related to what is happening outside the vehicle - at the things they see through the car window. But the dog can't reach them, so barks in frustration. Commonly, this barking will be directed at people and other dogs, but many dogs will also bark at cars, trucks, motorcycles, bicycles, children on skateboards, or at other animals, such as cats or horses.

The confined space of a car can make barking more likely, and more intense. Perhaps your dog feels trapped and is thus more reactive in a car. Or, alternatively, they may feel more secure, and that confidence makes them react more. Whatever the reason, it's common for many dogs to struggle to remain calm at the sight of various triggers on the other side of a car window.

Some dogs may bark when they see these same things in a different context—perhaps through the windows at home, or while out on walks. And dogs who react by barking in multiple situations often bark especially vigorously when in a car.

Car barking is irritating, frustrating and annoying. It's a common problem and potentially a significant safety concern, because it is highly distracting. Our roads are busy and dangerous enough without a deafening dog demanding your attention and reducing your reaction times.

What can I do to stop car barking?

Remember if you repeatedly shout "quiet!" or "no!" or "Shut UP!" when your dog is barking, you may be rewarding (and adding to) the behaviour rather than reducing it. Enough said.

There are only three options for dealing with any unwanted behaviour - ignore, prevent, or manage. Ignoring is impossible unless you have extremely good noise cancelling headphones, which are probably illegal to use when driving anyway. Although repeated exposure will mean you get habituated to it to some extent.

Prevention and management are often the easiest methods to try and can produce some startlingly quick results for some dogs.

1) Decide where your dog will travel

First, consider where and how your dog rides in the car. Dogs who move around inside a car can interfere with your ability to drive, or to see out of windows and will increase the risk of an accident simply from being a distraction.

Puppies often get car sick and can whine and yip. This usually resolves itself with time. Putting them in the centre of the car rather than a boot may help, but do seek vet help if your puppy is drooling, vomiting or eliminating.

I hope I don't need to remind you that dogs must be safely secured in the car, just like children. In the event of an accident, your unsecured dog can be seriously injured or killed, or might run off in terror straight in front of another vehicle. Loose dogs can kill front seat passengers and themselves, as a loose dog becomes a dangerous missile in a collision of any force.

Simply employing restraints such as a harness and seatbelt can help your dog feel more secure and more comfortable which may in itself reduce barking.

If there is room, a crate is an excellent management option. A well secured, well fitted, ventilated crate provides a safe and comfortable place for your dog to travel. Covering the crate with a blanket or rug can reduce or even eliminate barking at people, dogs and other triggers outside the vehicle by restricting your dogs' view. Especially if the crate can go on the back seat and you restrict their view to forwards only. But a covered crate in the boot is also a good option.

However this may not help a dog who is barking from anxiety as they might continue to bark.

2) Reducing movement triggers

Many dogs are triggered to bark because of seeing movement

through the side windows. An alternative to a crate is to cover the side windows with blinds, which can work well for some dogs. The blinds used as sunshades for children are not sufficient as they only diffuse sunlight rather than preventing your dog seeing out. You could try cutting blackout blind material to size then sticking it to the window with velcro tape so that it can easily be removed when you wish.

3) Calming measures

Another management option which can work well is to give your dog a yummy long lasting treat such as a filled Kong. This often works particularly well for dogs who bark from excitement or from anxiety, as by the time they have finished their treat you'll be well on your way, they'll be more relaxed and are then less likely to commence barking.

A head covering for your dog, such as a Thundercap, can also help. This will obscure your dog's vision without blocking it entirely. If you want to try this method, please teach your dog to be comfortable wearing it before using it on them in the car. Thundercaps can have a calming effect on many dogs in a variety of situations, including barking while in a car.

4) Train lie down and relax

Train your dog to lie down and remain in that position in the car, using a stuffed Kong or similar item to keep your dog occupied and relaxed. (If you don't have a solid down stay outside the car then teach that first.) Then start by practising a relaxed down with your car stationary in the driveway. Once your dog gets the hang of that, then take short journeys to other quiet places to practice.

With excitable, noisy canine passengers, the aim is to keep things calm. Make sure they are calm before getting in the car. Take your time coming out of your house and take time to settle your dog in the car before setting off. It can help to give them a chew to occupy them. When you get to your destination, wait in the car for your dog to be calm before allowing them out. Sit in the car with the windows slightly open, so your dog can sniff the scents and orient themselves. It's also a good idea (and a key safety action) to teach good car manners by asking your dog to "Wait" before getting into the car and also before being allowed to jump out.

5) Condition a positive response

For anxious dogs, your focus needs to be on helping them relax and enjoy car rides. Start by pairing the car with something your dog loves - a special treat or toy they only get when in the (stationary) car. Then add very short drives round your neighbourhood coming straight back home. Once your dog is happy with those, take them to a favourite place such as a local park or beach. The main goal of this is to get your dog looking forward to a ride in the car, instead of fearing it.

6) Barking at triggers

For dogs who bark at specific triggers when in the car, your first step is to work out exactly what it is that sets your dog off into their barking frenzy. Is it all people or just certain types? Is it all dogs or only those who are jumping around or barking themselves? Is it all other road vehicles or only specific ones such as motorbikes or those with throaty exhausts? Is it in specific circumstances, such as a vehicle overtaking you? Then you can make a plan.

Find somewhere where you know you are likely to see your dogs trigger(s) - car parks at busy beauty spots for people and dogs, or a town centre for vehicle triggers. Get in the back seat and simply praise your dog and give them a favourite, high value treat every time a trigger appears. It's worth keeping a special high value treat just for this training, such as the food your dog loves most. The aim is to link appearance of a trigger with you praising your dog then providing the special treat. Eventually, after more practice than you might think you'll need, your dog will start to look at you for their treat as soon as they spot a trigger.

The next stage is to add movement. For this you need someone else to be driving so you can continue to give your dog their treat whenever they see a trigger - it's not safe to try and combine this training with driving, for obvious reasons. Start with quieter places and few triggers and build up to more challenging areas. Once this behaviour is embedded, you can continue the training with you driving, as giving your dog praise when they see a trigger will predict their treat, which you can then toss them when it is safe to do so.

It's difficult, but important, to try and avoid car journeys where your dog will see triggers and can practice their barking while you are doing this training. If you live on your own or have no-one to help you with this prolonged training, then focus on the management options I've suggested instead.

Once I realised car barking was a problem with Gus, we tried various options - a covered crate, a dog tunnel, and covering the side windows. He hated being confined in the crate or tunnel when the car was moving, despite loving his indoor crate and being happy in the car crate when we were stationary. He barked when inside the covered area even more than before - and bit his way out on one long journey we had to do. I wish I'd started him in a car crate from the moment he arrived with us and taught him to lie down and relax in it.

Gus still barks in the car. He loves car journeys. His barking is mainly as a reaction to other cars moving, with an element of excitement and anticipation thrown in. I'm pretty sure he would be a car chaser if he ever got the chance - but we have always been careful never to let him off lead anywhere near moving cars. The barking is worst and most difficult to manage when a car is very close behind, or overtakes. I've half-taught him to stay lying down in the car (which does stop the barking), but I know I haven't done enough work on it. Mea culpa.

Interestingly Gus's barking seems to vary with which model and make of car he's in - we'd had three or four over the years. Some cars definitely encourage more barking than others. I'd be fascinated to know if you have found the same thing with your car barking dog. Please let me know!

Summary

- Barking in the car results from anxiety, excitement or frustration
- Prevention and management can produce quick results
- An established barking problem can be difficult to deal with
- Deal with the problem as early as possible

In the final chapter we'll talk about yet another form of nuisance barking, dogs who bark when out in the garden or backyard.

30

BARKING IN THE GARDEN OR YARD

I was sitting at my desk, typing away at some emails, with Gus snoozing on the floor beside me, when I heard a faint whirring sound in the distance. Gus lifted his head, then leapt to his feet and ran to the back door, stood on his hind legs to open it in his confident, effective manner, and shot outside, barking. The whirring sound had resolved itself into the chugging of a small light aircraft passing overhead. Gus ran in circles on the patio, barking until it had passed by. He trotted round, looking up, on patrol. There was a tiny silver flash as a jet flew miles overhead, followed by a pretty, puffy con-trail. Gus barked furiously again and my concentration was finally shattered.

I'm a dog trainer and behaviourist. I understand dogs and my brain is filled with all sorts of information about how to deal with unwanted behaviours.

But sometimes I forget to apply my knowledge to my own dog.

I love Gus, my rather hyper collie, to bits most of the time, but he drives me mad occasionally with his barking. If only I had dealt properly with it when he was a puppy…

Our house is just over the hill from the old Ballyhalbert airfield - we pulled up reams of copper wiring from the old approach lights when we created our garden from the field it was previously. The airfield was used regularly during the second World War, but has since fallen into disrepair. Half of it has been built on, however some of the old runway, taxiways and the old control tower ruins are still there.

Learner pilots from our local Newtownards airport use it for training to practice emergency approaches. They cut their engines and glide in towards the old runway, then, just before they reach it, they restart their engines to pull up and away. The engine restarts just happen to occur directly above our house. Then they circle round and do it all again, often two or three times in a row.

And they are at a low altitude when practising these manoeuvres.

It makes me jump, even though we've lived here for many years, because unless I'm outside I don't hear the silent, stealthy approach. Unsurprisingly, Gus, as a puppy, became very aroused by it and quickly started to bark at these noisy interlopers.

Stupidly, I did nothing much about it and just accepted he was as annoyed as I was by the disturbance. But then he started barking at any jets going over, too.

Still I did nothing. (Really stupid now.)

Then he started to bark at con trails. Now, I secretly admire him for this - it's pretty clever to work out that jet planes leave con trails, so con trails must mean that a plane is there even when he cannot see or hear it. But I wish he hadn't worked it out.

And this barking has become a habit. Worse, he gets a neuro-chemical buzz out of it, so it quickly became an addictive habit. It was the driver for him teaching himself how to open the back door so he could freely indulge in this behaviour. I should have acted far sooner.

Luckily, for most dogs, barking in the garden is far more mundane. Let's look at some reasons why this annoying behaviour happens.

Why do dogs bark in the garden?

One reason why dogs have been human companions for many thousands of years is that they are able to detect smells, noises and movements that we don't. A dog's ability to pick up the slightest change in the environment is uncanny. They are brilliant motion detectors, see far better in the dark than you can, and their scenting ability means they can detect creatures, birds, and other disturbances when you are oblivious to anything going on.

Added to that, dogs are natural predators. Many have been specifically bred to hunt small furry things, find and flush out birds, or attack intruders. This doesn't mean your canine companion always wants to kill anything that dares to move in your garden, but it does mean they are likely to become aroused and excited by wildlife, movement or noises nearby when out in your garden.

Dogs will alert you to someone approaching or passing by. You're probably happy to let your dog alert you to someone coming to visit, and to deter people from entering your property. But if your dog barks from your garden when someone approaches any neighbour's door in your street it doesn't usually go down well.

The final, and sadly common, reason dogs bark in the garden is through boredom or loneliness. I hope I needn't say that leaving your dog in the garden while you are out at work is a bad idea and almost always leads to a barking problem. Dogs are better left inside your home while you are out, with visits from family, friends or a dog walker if you're out for any length of time.

What can I do to stop my dog barking in the garden?

The easiest and first thing to do is to prevent the behaviour ever starting. I recommend not leaving your pup unsupervised in your garden at all for the first year - because that is the key time for habits to develop. (I allowed Gus to develop some bad habits in his first few months with us for all sorts of reasons I've outlined in my book *Chaos to Calmish: Diary of a Pesky Puppy's First Year*, but I would have saved myself a lot of heartache if I had dealt with his barking then.)

Leaving your dog outside to exercise and entertain themselves means they'll get up to mischief and look for things to do - and that's likely to include barking.

1) Prevention
Key prevention tips include:

1. Making sure you're there to supervise your puppy to stop any potential problems in their tracks - things like digging in your borders, discovering escape routes, eating poo and other unsavoury items, chasing birds or shadows, and, of course, barking

2. Ensuring your dog has sufficient mental stimulation and exercise from their other daily activities as described in previous chapters

But what if your dog has already developed a barking habit?

It can be difficult to change this behaviour, because you aren't in control of what comes into your garden or what passes by. If your dog is alone outside they will then make their own decisions about what to do, which is highly likely to include barking.

2) Identify triggers

Work out any key trigger times - school runs, rush hour, just after you've filled the bird food containers, mid morning when you know next door's cat comes to use your flower bed as their toilet, and so on. For Gus those times included 7.45-8am when the London flight passed over our house, and weekend afternoons when we're almost guaranteed to have light aircraft overhead. During those times, make sure your dog is safely in your house engaged in another activity.

3) Teach key cues

Next, teach your dog two vital obedience cues. The first is to teach "quiet" as described in chapter 23. Teaching an exceptional response to "quiet" involves teaching your dog first to bark, then training and proofing your "quiet" cue. But be careful using "quiet" to interrupt garden barking - it is all too easy to overuse the cue and reduce your dogs response to it.

The second is to teach a fantastic recall so you can call your dog away from a potential barking trigger.

These things will help prevent garden barking.

But perhaps you might need to manage and deal with an already established garden barking problem.

4) Dealing with garden barking

First, it may sound very obvious, but if your dog starts barking in the garden, bring them inside. Interrupting and preventing the practice of unwanted behaviours is key in addressing them. This includes never leaving your dog unattended outside.

When your dog needs to eliminate, attach them to a long lead and go out with them. Some dogs prefer to be on a Flexi or extending lead when eliminating as they stay more relaxed. But for training your dog not to bark in the garden you need an ordinary long lead or line.

Attach the long line whenever you allow your dog out into the garden: when you're going out to relax, or garden, or potter around. Every time. And watch your dog closely. Please don't think you can grab their collar - by the time you have reached your dog and managed to take hold of their collar they have already started to satisfy the barking urge. You need to be able to respond to the first bark, immediately.

As soon as they run towards their favourite barking spot, or alert to one of their triggers, or charge across the garden in preparation for a barking spree, use the line gently to break their onward movement then stop your dog using the line. Use your "Quiet" cue if necessary, and give your recall cue.

If your dog immediately responds and quietens, allow them to continue their garden perambulations. If not, use the line to bring them back to you and ask for a calming behaviour such as sit or down. Once they are calm, use a release cue such as "OK" or "Free" and allow them to wander off again. Repeat as necessary for as long as it takes to break the barking habit.

Another alternative is to use the line to take your dog back inside immediately and wait for them to be calm before going back outside again - though this can be a nuisance in wet and muddy weather.

Other things that can help include making sure your dog has plenty of activities to amuse them when outside, such as digging pits, food toys and sniffing areas. Do some training, create mini agility obstacles and sniff areas, and anything else that will entertain and amuse your dog and distract them from finding things to bark at.

~

If only I'd followed this advice with Gus.

Recently we were working with a client whose dog had been very frustrated, barking and lunging with other dogs. He had remained calm with Tippi and they had walked side by side happily. Next I brought Gus out. The owner and dog were doing really well and we had progressed to being just a few feet apart. Then Gus barked at a con trail, and the session deteriorated rapidly. Both dogs became very aroused, spinning and barking and took quite a few minutes to settle again. No real harm done, but it was an annoying and unnecessary interruption to a great training session.

If I had done something about Gus's barking at aircraft, or my study chair, or in the car, at the start, I might have stopped his barking becoming a habit and a problem, and saved myself many hours, months, days and years of training to control it.

Mea culpa.

Summary

- Always supervise your dog when they are out in your garden
- Intervene early to interrupt any barking
- Teach an excellent, reliable recall

Don't ignore the problem as I did. Use the suggestions in this book to prevent your dog learning this annoying habit so you and your neighbours can have a quieter, calmer life.

And please seek professional help from a good dog behaviourist if you're struggling with your dog.

AFTERWORD

I wrote this book to help owners who are struggling with these common problems. In my behaviour practice, fear and stress are at the root of 80-90% of the problems people seek help with. I specialised in helping dogs who are reactive and also dogs who hate being left alone, so I always knew I wanted to write about these issues.

My previous dogs barked very little, so Gus has been a revelation and a challenge. For most triggers, moving away and increasing distance is a key part of re-training the dog - but one can't increase distance from the sky....

Gus has also taught me humility. I understand just how hard it is to follow effective advice day by day when you are dealing with a problem behaviour. There are no magic bullets. I empathise with those who struggle with their dogs behaviour and take my hat off to all the people who work through their dog's issues successfully.

I hope this book has helped you understand your dog's behaviour better. Read on to discover some practical steps you can take for further help.

31

NEXT STEPS

Perhaps you'd like to know more, or find some help about specific problems you're facing with your dog? I can only include general advice in any book.

Here's some things that will help:

1) Go to the website, www.downdog.co.uk, to download a free booklet: **How To Find Your Dog's Kryptonite.**

You will:

* Discover the FIVE magic rewards your dog will love

* Learn how to ask your dog what they want - so they'll do what you want. Because training is not all about giving food treats.

All delivered to you by t'internet pixies

2) The website has plenty of free help sheets and videos, and my blog, where you can find a range of articles on a variety of topics.

3) I've produced online courses covering a wide range of topics, from general training to specialised help - visit online.downdog.co.uk to find out more.

4) If you feel you need help now, please look for an accredited behaviourist. Ask them about their training and qualifications and request testimonials from other clients.

5) Buy my other books. They're available in paperback or Kindle

versions or you can get them for free through Kindle Unlimited. Here's a brief synopsis:

Pesky Puppy to Perfect Pet

From considering getting a puppy or new dog through the manic first few weeks, this book is a puppy bible for new owners, covering what to do about those pesky puppy problems as well as the essential socialisation and training you need to do so you'll have the perfect pet you always wanted.

Chaos to Calmish: Diary of a Pesky Puppy's First Year

This is the honest, contemporaneous diary of the first year of Gus's life, to show, warts and all, what life is like day-to-day with a new puppy. It describes the things I did well and explains where I could have done things better. I'm honest about the mistakes I made and how readers can avoid them. And it's got plenty of lovely pictures of my gorgeous Gus.

Problem Pooch Book 1: Troublesome to Tranquil

The first book in the three-book Problem Pooch series covers sixteen common problem behaviours you might face in and around the home. I explain the possible reasons why your dog might choose to act in that way, then give you a range of tips you can try to change that unwanted behaviour in your own dog.

HELP! How to socialise your puppy

This book gives you easy to follow, practical advice and tips on how to socialise your new puppy when you can't get out much, or at all, due to life limitations. The advice applies at 'normal' times too.

Please may I have a puppy?

This book, aimed especially at children aged 6-14, will tell you what you need to know before getting a puppy, how to choose the right puppy, what to do from the day you bring them home and what you need to teach your puppy to be your perfect pet.

Doggy Doctor Surgery Secrets

This book tells my story - about how working as a doctor helped me become a leading dog trainer and behaviourist, The Doggy

Doctor and how this makes me uniquely positioned to help others wanting to become dog trainers. In it, I share how my experience in medicine can help people build their knowledge, confidence and skills to become effective, empathetic dog professionals in their own right.

ABOUT THE AUTHOR

Carol set up Down Dog Training and Behaviour in 2008 although she's has been training people and their Perfect Pets for nearly 40 years now (she started young).

Carol, The Doggy Doctor, is based in Northern Ireland. She has the honour to be the first Kennel Club Accredited Instructor for Companion Dog training (at advanced level) in Northern Ireland and the first (and currently only) Kennel Club Accredited Instructor in Behavioural Training in Ireland. She holds the Advanced Diploma in Canine Behaviour Management (with Distinction), is a Guild of Dog Trainers Master Trainer (GoDT 138) and is a Qualified International Dog Training Instructor.

She's passionate about helping owners and their problem pooches and also helps people who want to become dog trainers or dog behaviourists. After a long and successful career, she is retiring in summer 2022.

But she's not just about dogs. She set up her dog business originally to help fund her craft and book addictions. She enjoys a range of crafts for relaxation, including card-making (as Crafty Carol, https://craftycarolscards.co.uk) and bobbin lace. She's an avid reader and has far too many books, according to Himself. And that doesn't include the thousands of books on her Kindle account…

Six years ago she started writing her own books and now has seven, with an eight and ninth in progress. One day she'd like to write a novel, too.

COMING SOON

P roblem Pooch to Perfect Pet Book 3: (title to be finalised)
This third volume in this series covers medical factors
that can lead to behaviour problems and deals with
aggression in all its varied forms, including to people and to other
dogs.

Doggy Doctor: More Surgery Secrets
More tales from the surgery that have helped me to deal with
dog owners and their problem dogs and why dog trainers are
actually human trainers.

ACKNOWLEDGMENTS

Writing a book is hard work. This is my seventh book - but it doesn't get any easier. I often fight to find two words to link together and those pithy phrases I think of in the middle of the night in bed vanish like Cinderella's carriage and horses as soon as I assume a vertical position.

The book suffered a long delay between being finished and being published because sadly, my brother died suddenly and unexpectedly on the very day of my deadline for comments from my beta readers. Thank you all for being so patient.

I couldn't have written this book without the staunch support of several wonderful people.

First, thanks to Gareth, who has been my right-hand man at Down Dog for many years. Thank you for everything you've done, coping with me bombarding you with new ideas and website changes, as well as leading all the training classes. Thank you for being there when I need to talk things through and thank you for doing the wonderful covers for my books too. I wish you every success with your new business, The Campus.

Huge thanks too to Vicky Quinn-Fraser of Moxie books (moxiebooks.co.uk). Vicky, you've given me belief, support and shedloads of practical help. Your Moxie Books membership group, the daily Power Hours and the Write Nights have made writing so much easier. I doubt this book would ever have been finished without you. Heartfelt thanks.

Thanks also to my pet dog Biz Wiz gooroo, Dom Hodgson, of

growyourpetbusinessfast.com. His no-nonsense, straight talking help and support was sometimes hard to take but he never stopped pushing me to develop further. He kept my nose to the grindstone when I was tempted to sit back on my laurels. Thanks Dom. You're just great.

Last but not least, thanks to my long-suffering husband, David aka Himself, who quietly puts up with my self-imposed pressure tetchiness when things aren't going as I want them to. He often starred in my emails and takes being recognised as "Himself" with good grace. He does so much in the background to support me, from taking Gus for walks, to arranging his own life around my other commitments. He's always there for me when things are tough. David, you have no idea how much I need and love you. Thank you from the bottom of my heart.

You're all amazing and I couldn't do what I've done without you. Thank you all.

Printed in Great Britain
by Amazon

40925832R00159